M000034564

On college campuses across the US today, I frequently encounter the objections that Christianity is sexist, and the Bible is bad news for women. In this devotional, Ann White compellingly and compassionately demonstrates that the Bible is inhabited by strong and courageous women, and the Christian God consistently calls, encourages, and equips women—in the Bible, throughout history, and today! Studying and praying through this devotional has not only renewed my gratitude that God has adopted me into His family as His daughter, but it has also impressed upon me afresh why Jesus is exactly the kind of man I want to spend time with and exactly the kind of God I long to worship.

—*Jo Vitale, dean of studies, Zacharias Institute*

What courageous life are you being called to? If you need encouragement for strength, commit ninety days to *She Is Strong and Courageous*. In this book, you will read stories of courageous women and be prepared to pursue and live your own call to courage.

—*Dee Ann Turner, retired vice president of Chick-fil-A, and best-selling author of* It's My Pleasure

By sharing the lives of numerous women in the Bible and the history of the world, Ann White compels us to reach for strength and courage. As women uniquely created by God for His purposes and pleasure, these devotions bolster our convictions as we impact our circles of influence. Ann's personal struggles served as a catalyst for empowering women to reach beyond themselves to grasp their God-given missions. May each of us embrace the journey with renewed expectations of what God will do in and through us!

—*Mary Perdue, former first lady of Georgia*

Today, we need examples of courageous women because our culture broadcasts messages that we aren't pretty enough, smart enough, or good enough, which is why Ann White has had enough. Here's a woman who is taking a stand to mentor other women in leading, risk-taking, and living out our faith in the face of adversity. *She Is Strong and Courageous* will educate and inspire you to become all that God has called you to be and to find genuine contentment in life. It's time to take a stand. Buy a copy for yourself and another to give to a girlfriend, family member, or someone else who needs courage for life. You'll never regret it.

—*Kathleen Cooke, co-founder of Cooke Pictures and The Influence Lab, and author of* Hope 4 Today: Staying Connected to God in a Distracted Culture

God has developed a magnificent ministry in Courage for Life. Ann White's new book, *She Is Strong and Courageous,* will help you build a bold, positive, faithful lifestyle that will overcome the fear, stress, and pressure of life that we women all face!

—*Trudy Davies Davis, RN, certified style professional, media personality, and Mrs. Georgia International 2013*

This is a devotional I will read again and again. So simple to read yet profound in its application for real-time living. *She Is Strong and Courageous* could easily be utilized as a women's Bible study tool. Ann shares so much depth without too many complicated cross references or comparisons. The way she has compressed the principals without compromising Scripture or context is something anyone can grasp. A devotional for anyone, anywhere that does not intimidate or confuse.

—*Sabrina Pinion, Mrs. Universe 2014*

*She Is Strong and Courageous* by Ann White is an anointed collection and study of some of the most inspirational women in history. God has simply breathed a masterpiece on the pages of this book to grow us each day. Ann lives what she teaches and is an example of strength and courage to me personally, as a friend, prayer partner, and television co-host. God has raised Ann up for such a time as this with a message of courage for the Body of Christ. I highly recommend this devotional for every person who desires to press past all boundaries and limitations of fear to fulfill the call of God on her life.

—*Rebecca Keener, president of Heritage Christian Fellowship, Inc., host of* Always More TV, *and co-host of* The Christian View

Prepare to be inspired by these female faith warriors! From Naomi's Ruth to Billy Graham's Ruth, their stories really are our stories. I cannot wait to share this book with the many women in my life who, like me, always seem to be in need of courage.

—*Kimberley Kennedy, television host and author of* Left at the Altar

*She Is Strong and Courageous* is an inspiring book overflowing with biblical examples of women who stepped out in courage to fulfill their calling and mission. Read this book and learn from some of the most courageous Christian women in history.

—*Jennifer Stovall Eichelberger, television producer for WATC-TV, and licensed and ordained minister*

Whether you're looking for timeless truths or encouraging examples, Ann White has written a wonderful book that provides biblical wisdom and thought-provoking application about courage and strength. Grab a copy and grab a highlighter!

—*Holly M. Duncan, licensed professional counselor and CEO of Parkridge*

Expounding through the legacy of heroic leadership of women from the Bible, the twentieth century, and today, *She Is Strong and Courageous* takes you on a daily journey to challenge and enlighten your endeavor to strive for greater strength.

—*Marcylle Combs, president and owner of Foundation Management Services*

*She Is Strong and Courageous* is a refreshing and inspiring look at extraordinary women who have made a difference in our world. A courage warrior in her own right, God has called Ann White to speak words of biblical truth and wisdom in masterful ways that can transform our faith and empower us to press on in spiritual strength and perseverance.

— *Allison Bottke, bestselling author of the* Setting Boundaries *series and* God Allows U-Turns *anthology*

*She is*

# STRONG

*and*

# COURAGEOUS

A 90-Day Devotional

ANN WHITE

**BroadStreet**
PUBLISHING

BroadStreet Publishing® Group, LLC
Savage, Minnesota, USA
BroadStreetPublishing.com

# SHE IS STRONG AND COURAGEOUS: A 90-Day Devotional

978-1-4245-5751-6 (faux leather)
978-1-4245-5752-3 (e-book)

Stock or custom editions of BroadStreet Publishing titles may be purchased in bulk for educational, business, ministry, fundraising, or sales promotional use. For information, please email info@ broadstreetpublishing.com.

Cover and interior design by Chris Garborg at garborgdesign.com
Typesetting by Kjell Garborg at garborgdesign.com

Printed in China
18 19 20 21 22 5 4 3 2 1

To every courageous Christian woman who remains faithful to God in times of opposition and perseveres in a world that seeks to hold you back — your legacy inspires us all to be strong and courageous as we embrace our God-given calling and pursue our God-given dreams.

"Do not fear, for I am with you; do not anxiously look about you, for I am your God. I will strengthen you, surely I will help you, surely I will uphold you with My righteous right hand."

ISAIAH 41:10 NASB

# CONTENTS

# INTRODUCTION

Our minds shape our belief systems about family, love, marriage, God, and life as we experience it. These beliefs, in turn, shape our choices and habits, both good and bad.

God's desire is to enable us to make healthy choices that honor him first, and subsequently, the hope and wholeness he can give will flow through us and into all our life and relationships. He wants our lives to be healthy, to come from places of truth. He wants us to walk in power and purpose—to embrace our God-given courage to pursue our God-given dreams.

Have you ever been so fearful of losing something or someone that you found yourself doing things you didn't really want to do?

Most of my life was worrying about what others wanted, wished, or thought of me. As a result of childhood experiences, I was terrified of rejection and, for years, I put my relationship with God aside in order to focus on others and myself. But God didn't want me to put my relationship with him aside. He wanted me to grow to a place where an honest and loving relationship with him would take precedence in my life and become the central beat of my heart. He wanted me to completely grasp the depth of his love for me in order that I might fall deeper in love with him.

When I didn't have enough courage to "obey God rather than men,"

God didn't give up on me. He continued to work with me and directed my path toward a resolution that helped me move forward—he drew me into an in-depth study of his Word; where I began to deposit truth that helped to drown out the lies. The more I studied, the hungrier I became. Once God's Word really takes hold of your heart, it's hard to contain the passion.

God doesn't want to be contained and controlled. He doesn't want us to live a double-standard life. God's desire is to draw us closer to him where we can draw from his unlimited supply of courage to face life's challenges and our calling with unwavering bravery.

## Finding Courage

Courage is something most of us want. It's an attribute that encourages us to venture outside our comfort zone and embrace the possibilities. It gives us the ability to be brave, to conquer fear and despair so we can take on necessary challenges and make necessary changes.

The Hebrew word for courage is *hāzaq*, which literally means "to show oneself strong," and it appears numerous times in Scripture. The Bible provides many rich examples of courage. Throughout God's Word, we see miraculous accounts of God accomplishing great deeds through ordinary people.

Having courage is, in essence, all about making good decisions— God decisions.

Throughout this devotion, together we will explore the courageous spirits of women of the Bible, women throughout history, and women in our world today who inspire us to be strong and courageous in our walk with God and throughout life's twists and turns.

## Pursuing Knowledge

Hosea 4:6 reads, "My people are destroyed for lack of knowledge" (NIV). Knowledge broadens our potential, then transforms our ability when we put it into practice.

God, in his abundant love for you and me, gives us the opportunity to learn invaluable life lessons through his written Word. In it, he reveals his character, so we might come to know him more and his relationship with mankind more personally, so we might understand him more fully. The Bible is profitable for our instruction, correction, and training, so we might be adequately prepared to face the various aspects of our everyday lives (2 Timothy 3:16). Without reading, grasping, and applying its truth to our lives on a regular basis, we set ourselves up for a fall.

The key to allowing God's Word to impact our everyday lives hinges on how and how often we approach it. According to the Center for Bible Engagement, there is direct correlation between the amount of time we spend in God's Word and the state of our behavior. We must set aside time to read the Bible and strive for an accurate interpretation of Scripture if we want to embrace the abundant life Christ has made available (John 10:10).

Before being introduced to a process of how to study the Bible, I relied on sermons, Sunday school lessons, commentaries, and dialogue with Christian friends for my knowledge and understanding of God's Word. While these resources are often valuable and reliable, they should never take the place of a dedication to reading and studying the Bible for ourselves.

In 2006, I began studying God's Word consistently. After more than a decade, I have fallen in love with the study of Scripture and experienced firsthand the value of being able to discern God's truth for myself.

There are four basic Bible study steps I implement every time I read or study God's Word.

1. **Pray** — Ask the Holy Spirit to guide you into all truth.
2. **Observe** — Ask the question: What does the passage say?
3. **Interpret** — Ask the question: What timeless life lesson does the passage teach?
4. **Apply** — Ask the question: What do I need to do to apply the lesson to my life?

## Influence

*She Is Strong and Courageous* is the result of countless hours of research and examination of the lives and influence of courageous women of faith. Throughout this devotion, we will explore the courageous spirit of women of the Bible, women throughout history, and women in our world today. Strong and courageous women who motivate us to embrace our God-given courage and pursue our God-given dreams.

Together, we will find the courage our souls desperately long for. We will stand firm, not hampered or weighed down by the burdens the world seeks to place on us. As fellow warriors, we will learn how to lay aside our heavy loads to take up Christ's yoke that is far lighter (Matthew 11:29-30). Together, we will learn how to make fearless choices and walk in grace. Together, we will find the courage to change our lives.

Could it be you are reading this today as part of God's plan, as an answer to prayer? God wants you to be courageous. And he wants you to embrace his love and grace and experience the abundant life he makes available to each and every one of us.

My prayer is that you too, just as I have, will gain inspiration, courage, and confidence from the accounts of the courageous women of God who are celebrated in this devotional. These are women who've courageously traversed life's peaks and valleys before us. We can draw strength from their legacies of influence, as we strive to make fearless choices, walk in grace, and embrace courage for life.

*Day 1*

# MAKE COURAGEOUS COMMITMENTS

## (RUTH)

But Ruth replied, "Don't ask me to leave you and turn back.
Wherever you go, I will go; wherever you live, I will live.
Your people will be my people, and your God will be my God.
Wherever you die, I will die, and there I will be buried.
May the Lord punish me severely if I allow anything but death
to separate us!" When Naomi saw that Ruth was determined
to go with her, she said nothing more.

Ruth 1:16–18

*Pray*

*Lord, open my eyes to your truth and help me
understand and obey your precepts.*

*Observe*

Each day, we are given twenty-four hours to work
with. But we often try to squeeze something into every
crevice of our day, leaving only enough time to sleep, so
we can get up tomorrow and do it all over again.

When making commitments, we need to be
mindful of where they fit into our overall goals,
objectives, and schedules. And we must consider how
they fit into God's overall plan and purpose for our lives.

Once we've prayerfully considered these factors and are confident in our chosen direction, we must then avoid procrastination and take action. All the while, we should be diligent to analyze and prioritize our commitments on a regular basis, avoiding anxiety and maintaining balance in our everyday lives and schedules.

In the book of Ruth, we encounter a daughter-in-law who boldly makes a life-changing commitment to her deceased husband's mother. Ruth had married into a family that worshiped the one true God, and when it came time for her to make the choice to return to her family and the gods they served or travel with her mother-in-law to an unfamiliar land, she chose her commitment wisely.

Courageously analyze and prioritize your commitments by asking yourself the following questions.

1. What commitments have I made?
2. What commitments do I need to make?
3. Are there any commitments I need to eliminate?
4. How dedicated am I to my commitments?

Prayerfully analyzing your commitments can mean the difference between success and defeat, peace of mind and exhaustion.

### Interpret

God will give us everything we need to make courageous, God-honoring commitments. He promises to be with us along the way and will bless us in response to our dedication.

### Apply

Analyze and prioritize your commitments today. Make the ones God is encouraging you to make, eliminate the ones he's encouraging you to eliminate, put aside procrastination, and take action.

### Pray

*Father, give me wisdom and discernment regarding my commitments. Help me discern areas of my life where I am overcommitted or under committed. Grant me the ability to eliminate commitments that are not within your will and establish ones that honor you.*

## Day 2

# CHOOSE CHARACTER
# OVER COMPROMISE

### (ABIGAIL)

Abigail wasted no time. She quickly gathered 200 loaves of bread, two wineskins full of wine, five sheep that had been slaughtered, nearly a bushel of roasted grain, 100 clusters of raisins, and 200 fig cakes. She packed them on donkeys and said to her servants, "Go on ahead. I will follow you shortly."

1 SAMUEL 25:18–19

### Pray

*Lord, enlighten my mind with truth as I seek inspiration and guidance from your Word.*

### Observe

Popular culture places achieving goals over faithfulness to God. It takes courage to stand up for our faith and choose character over achievement.

We live in a world that promotes compromise, that says, "Do whatever is necessary to accomplish your goals and meet your needs—even if it means disregarding your convictions." When we read the biblical account of Abigail and Nabal in 1 Samuel

25:1–42, we observe a husband and wife with very different views on integrity. While Nabal was harsh and evil in his dealings, Abigail remained a loyal wife, yet refused to compromise when it came to honoring God's calling to care for the needs of David's men. She was strong and courageous in her faithfulness.

We must regularly examine our motives and ask ourselves: *Is it more important for me to achieve my goals and meet my earthly desires than to value God's calling and my character?*

Abigail was a noble woman whose husband's distinguishing characteristic was his ill-tempered attitude. Desiring to please God and with many lives at stake, she courageously chose to provide for David and his men.

Courageously maintain your integrity by practicing the following.

1. **Think before you speak and act.** Think about what you are thinking, consider how and what you are saying, and always objectively appraise each situation before you act.
2. **Be accountable.** Invite safe friends to inspect your life, to challenge you in maintaining your integrity. Give them permission to hold you accountable.

3. **Be honest.** Be upfront, truthful, and willing to admit when you've made a mistake or done something wrong.
4. **Seek to please God.** Base your decisions on what God thinks and not on what the world thinks.

## Interpret

God is pleased when we choose faithfulness to him over our own personal desires and achievements.

## Apply

What area of your life are you most vulnerable to compromise? What specific plan can you put in place today to maintain and protect your devotion to godly character?

## Pray

*Father, protect me from compromise. Help me guard my heart and mind from being enticed by worldly possessions. And give me the ability to strive for Christ-like behavior in everything I do.*

# Day 3

# BE RESOLUTE

## (ROSA PARKS)

Be on guard. Stand firm in the faith. Be courageous. Be strong.
And do everything with love.

1 Corinthians 16:13–14

## Pray

*Lord, open the eyes of my heart and help me discern truth from your Word.*

## Observe

We all make commitments to do—or not to do certain things throughout our lives. Unfortunately, many of our commitments fall by the wayside within thirty days of making them. When we're put to the test and worldly pressure intensifies, we are subject to cave and back down from our cause.

So what will it take to help us remain resolute?

When our resolutions are ones that honor God, he will help us keep them. God directs our path, supports our efforts, and gives us everything we need to stand firm in our commitments. God's Word encourages us repeatedly to examine our ways (Lamentations 3:40;

1 Corinthians 11:28), be strong and courageous (Joshua 1:9; 2), do not fear (Isaiah 41:10), *and* not to give up (Galatians 6:9; Romans 5:3-5). Scripture also teaches us to hold one another accountable (1 Thessalonians 5:11; Ecclesiastes 4:9-10).

In 1955, Rosa Parks politely refused to give up her seat on a city bus in Montgomery, Alabama. In doing so, she took a stand against racial discrimination and ultimately helped initiate the civil rights movement in the United States. Over the next fifty years, Rosa became a nationally recognized symbol of courage and determination in the struggle to end racial segregation.

> "When that white driver stepped back toward us, when he waved his hand and ordered us up and out of our seats, I felt a determination cover my body like a quilt on a winter night." —Rosa Parks

When we keep our eyes on Christ and allow him to be the source of our strength, we become an instrument in God's hands and can even change the course of history.

Courageously stand resolute in your faith by exercising the following attributes.

1. Evaluate your commitments and position to ensure they are godly and necessary.

2. Embrace your God-given courage and face your challenges, even if you're afraid.
3. Persevere and press on to overcome any obstacle standing in your way.
4. Rely on the support of Godly friends and loved ones to encourage and support you.

## Interpret

God expects us to be strong and courageous in everything he calls us to do.

## Apply

Begin memorizing Philippians 4:13 and allow this passage to inspire you to be resolute in sharing your faith with someone today.

## Pray

*Father, thank you for giving me the ability to be brave when you call me to be take a stand. Please help me to honor you, stand firm in my faith, and represent you well.*

# MAINTAIN A FAITH-FILLED ATTITUDE

## (ESTHER)

Then Esther sent this reply to Mordecai: "Go and gather together all the Jews of Susa and fast for me. Do not eat or drink for three days, night or day. My maids and I will do the same. And then, though it is against the law, I will go in to see the king. If I must die, I must die."

ESTHER 4:15–16

## Pray

*Lord, remove my distractions and help me focus on truth from your Word.*

## Observe

Our attitudes and choices reveal the depth of our commitment to God.

Faith is taking God at his word. It's believing he is all-powerful, all-knowing, ever-present, faithful, and true. It's seen in our perspectives and attitudes. It is a mindset that God inspires us to pursue as we study the accounts of godly men and women who have gone before us. Esther, for example, was a courageous Hebrew woman whom God commissioned to deliver the nation of Israel. In her heroic story, found in the book of Esther, we discover Xerxes, king of Persia, chose her to be his queen.

Although Esther was admired by everyone who saw her (Esther 2:15) and loved by the king more than any other woman (Esther 2:17), she never allowed royalty and favor to impact her stellar character. Throughout the account of the Jews, frightening ordeal, Esther consistently displayed a gentle, merciful, humble, and courageous attitude.

In Matthew 5:1–12, most commonly referred to as the Beatitudes, Jesus describes eight attitudes we are to pursue, ones Esther exemplified beautifully.

Courageously maintain a faith-filled attitude by practicing the following Beatitudes.

1. **Humility**. Be humbly aware that you are spiritually bankrupt without Christ.
2. **Sorrow**. Be mournful over your sin and the moral decay in our world.
3. **Gentleness**. Be gentle as you respond and relate to others.
4. **Desperation**. Hunger and thirst in your pursuit of Christ-like behavior.
5. **Mercy**. Be generous and compassionate toward others in need.

6. **Morality**. Strive for moral purity in your thoughts and actions.
7. **Harmony**. Be peacemakers who desire wholeness in broken relationships.
8. **Perseverance**. Stand firm in your faith even when you are persecuted.

*Interpret*

As Christ-followers, we are to strive to maintain these attitudes, and in return we will receive the blessings associated with each one.

*Apply*

Which of the eight Beatitudes do you struggle to maintain? Pray and ask God to help you in courageously exercising this attitude today.

*Pray*

*Father, give me the strength to be authentic in my walk with you and the courage to be faithful in my pursuit of righteousness. I am forever grateful you give me the ability to persevere and extend mercy to me each time I fall short.*

# SHARE TRUTH WITH OTHERS

## (WOMAN AT THE WELL)

The woman said, "I know the Messiah is coming—the one who is called Christ. When he comes, he will explain everything to us." Then Jesus told her, "I AM the Messiah!" … The woman left her water jar beside the well and ran back to the village, telling everyone.

JOHN 4:25–26, 28

## *Pray*

*Lord, let me clearly observe truth in your Word and properly apply it to my life.*

## *Observe*

When we've learned something we are excited about, we want to tell others. When we discover a better way of doing things, we want to show others. And when we experience a life change, we can't wait to share our encounter in hopes others will experience it too.

Our primary biblical command is to "go and make disciples of all the nations" (Matthew 28:19). Yet sharing our salvation can be one of the hardest experiences to share—often because we're afraid. We fear conflict or challenges from non-believers; we fear others will disapprove of our stance; we fear we simply don't know enough. And sometimes we fear others won't believe us because of our past. We must regularly challenge ourselves to overcome our fears.

None of these excuses kept the woman of Samaria from sharing her faith. In Luke chapter 4, we read of Jesus' encounter with a woman at Jacob's well. This woman was a sinner, shamed by her lifestyle, drawing water at a time of day when no others were around. But on that day, she met the Messiah, who changed her life forever. In response and in spite of her reputation, she boldly ran back to her village to tell "everyone." She was strong and courageous, as she became the first woman evangelist of the city of Samaria.

Courageously share your faith by practicing the following.

1. Pray and ask God to give you the courage and opportunity to share your faith.
2. Be aware at all times of others in need of encouragement.
3. Practice sharing your faith by sharing it with someone you feel safe with, like a family member or close friend.

4. Put aside any hesitation and start a conversation with someone by asking how you can pray for him or her.

## Interpret

We are strong and courageous when we overcome our fears and choose to share our faith.

## Apply

Will you share your faith today? Look for opportunities to tell others about the hope you have found. The more you practice, the easier it becomes.

## Pray

*Father, open my eyes to the needs of others and give me the courage to share my faith. Help me boldly tell of your life-saving grace and the hope that's available as we surrender to you.*

*Day 6*

# HAVE COMPASSION

## (RUTH BELL GRAHAM)

Therefore, as God's chosen people, holy and dearly loved,
clothe yourselves with compassion, kindness, humility,
gentleness and patience. Bear with each other and forgive one
another if any of you has a grievance against someone else.
Forgive as the Lord forgave you.

Colossians 3:12–13 NIV

*Pray*

*Lord, sensitize me to others and their needs.*

*Observe*

Is God challenging you to adjust your outlook or
attitude? When we adopt a positive attitude, it directly
impacts our outlook, personalities, and relationships.
With our busy schedules and multitudes of distractions,
we rarely stop to consider what's going on in the lives
of others. When we intentionally slow down and
observe the world around us, we can see more clearly
the struggles and challenges many are facing.

Are you simply being polite when you bump into a
co-worker, friend, or loved one and ask, "How are you?"

Or do you really want to know? Have you ever been asked that question, only to realize the person asking really doesn't care about the answer?

When we take the time to ask people how they are doing and genuinely listen to and care about their response, we gain a more realistic perspective of the person's circumstances and put ourselves in a better position to feel and show compassion.

Wife of evangelist Billy Graham, Ruth Bell Graham, was known to be the glue that held the Graham family together. It's said she modeled Christ-like compassion and would happily give someone the dress off her back. In fact, that's exactly what she did. During a world evangelism conference, Ruth found a change of clothes and gave an African pastor the dress she was wearing when he mentioned he just couldn't return home without bringing his wife a gift.

Courageously exercise compassion by putting the following into practice.

1. **Set aside judgment**. When someone is curt, arrogant, or downright mean, consider what difficulty he or she may be facing and offer to pray for him or her.
2. **Accept differences**. We all come from different backgrounds, upbringing, life

experiences, and levels of spiritual growth. Therefore, strive to be considerate of your differences.

3. **Ask and listen attentively**. Ask at least one person each day, "How are you?" Listen attentively to his or her answer.

4. **Actively express compassion**. Openly express compassion for others by giving of your time, talents, or resources.

## Interpret

God expects us to be compassionate, kind, humble, gentle, patient, and forgiving toward others.

## Apply

Write down one way you can show compassion to others today and exercise compassion by implementing it throughout the day.

## Pray

*Father, thank you for your never-ending love, compassion, and patience toward me. Please help me recognize the needs of others and genuinely express true compassion toward them.*

# EMBRACE OPPORTUNITIES

## (LYDIA)

On the Sabbath we went a little way outside the city to a riverbank, where we thought people would be meeting for prayer, and we sat down to speak with some women who had gathered there. One of them was Lydia from Thyatira, a merchant of expensive purple cloth, who worshiped God. As she listened to us, the Lord opened her heart, and she accepted what Paul was saying. … When Paul and Silas left the prison, they returned to the home of Lydia. There they met with the believers and encouraged them once more. Then they left town.

ACTS 16:13–14, 40

*Pray*

*Lord, help me to be a doer of your Word and not just a hearer.*

*Observe*

Too often, we allow fear to be a determining factor in our decisions. Maybe you're ready for a career change, in need of medical treatment, or desire to pursue healthier relationships. Or maybe God is calling you to step out of your comfort zone and serve him in a specific way. The reality is, no matter what action God calls us to embrace, we all need God-given courage to take that first step.

When God opens doors for us, he won't leave us alone to face the challenge. God promises to work in and through us, giving us everything we need to accomplish our God-given tasks—if we choose to lean into his guiding and providing hands (Ephesians 3:20).

Lydia, a prominent businesswoman of Thyatira, heard the apostle Paul preach the gospel and seized the opportunity to receive Christ as her savior. She publically confessed her faith and was baptized. Then she immediately began sharing her testimony, and her entire household was saved. Lydia embraced the opportunity to become Paul's first European convert and accepted God's calling to lead others to saving faith in Christ and to open her home as a gathering place for believers.

Is there an opportunity or challenge God is encouraging you to accept? If so, what is holding you back?

Courageously embrace your God-given opportunities by practicing the following steps.

1. Identify your God-given opportunities.
2. Pinpoint any challenges keeping you from embracing the possibilities.

3. Ask friends and loved ones for support.
4. Determine the necessary steps and take action.

## Interpret

When God opens our hearts to an opportunity, he expects us to embrace it and will give us everything we need to accomplish the task.

## Apply

What opportunity is God calling you to embrace? Name one step you can take today to engage this opportunity.

## Pray

*Father, thank you for opening doors that challenge me to step out of my comfort zone and follow you. Help me know the steps you are calling me to take and give me courage to take them.*

# INCORPORATE DISCIPLESHIP

## (LOIS AND EUNICE)

I remember your genuine faith, for you share the faith that first filled your grandmother Lois and your mother, Eunice. And I know that same faith continues strong in you. This is why I remind you to fan into flames the spiritual gift God gave you when I laid my hands on you. For God has not given us a spirit of fear and timidity, but of power, love, and self-discipline. So never be ashamed to tell others about our Lord.

2 TIMOTHY 1:5–8

*Pray*

*Lord, open the eyes of my heart and help me discern truth from your Word.*

*Observe*

Discipleship, as modeled by Christ, consists of "doing life" together. When we freely share our faith and experiences with others, we help them navigate their spiritual journey with more courage and confidence. The Christian walk is one of continually striving to be more like Christ, and it's much more difficult to navigate when we attempt to do it alone.

Eunice, along with her mother, Lois, had a

profound spiritual influence on young Timothy. Because of their spiritual guidance, Timothy had a "genuine faith" and was well prepared to become the apostle Paul's most trusted companion and an influential evangelist. These two godly women valued the responsibility of courageously passing their faith on to the next generation.

We too must strive to intentionally engage in discipleship. Both by helping younger believers grow spiritually, and by inviting more mature believers to disciple us.

Consider the following scenarios and courageously pursue discipleship.

1. If you've recently surrendered your life to Christ, you can disciple others by sharing the Gospel and your testimony of how you came to know God.

2. If you've just started reading your Bible, you can disciple others by sharing what you're learning and encourage them to learn along with you.

3. If you're more mature in your faith, you've got a lot to share—from your knowledge of God's Word to the mistakes you've made along the way.

## Interpret

We must embrace our responsibility to share our faith with others and encourage others in their spiritual walk with God.

## Apply

Have you considered how much you have to offer to someone who is newer in his or her faith? Do you recognize your need to be discipled? Write down the name of one person you will offer to disciple and the name of one person you will ask to disciple you.

## Pray

*Father, help me fully realize my need for discipleship; make it clear to me the people in my life I need to disciple and those I need to be discipled by. Then give me the determination and courage to reach out and implement discipleship relationships.*

# WALK WITH GOD

## (MOTHER THERESA)

O people, the LORD has told you what is good, and this is what he requires of you: to do what is right, to love mercy, and to walk humbly with your God.

MICAH 6:8

## Pray

*Lord, open my eyes to your truth and help me understand and obey your precepts.*

## Observe

Do you ever stop to think about what it means to walk with God?

When we walk with someone, we spend time getting to know that person; we take the time to ask and answer questions; we listen attentively to that individual's point of view, and we are interested in her or her life. The same is true when we walk with God.

In Genesis 5:21–24 and 2 Kings 2:11, we read of two faithful followers who devoted their lives to walking with God. They walked with God so closely that He "took them," in lieu of them having to experience a physical death. God possibly said, "You've walked alongside me for so long now, you might as well walk on home with me."

When we sincerely walk with God, he requires us to do what is right, to love mercy, and walk humbly.

Mother Teresa inspires us by her courageous walk with the Lord. Her love for God was poured out on others through her compassionate love for the world's poor. She was a world-renowned peacemaker and a Nobel Peace Prize recipient. She was considered one of the twentieth century's greatest humanitarians who walked and lived among the poorest of the poor. Mother Teresa's love for the Lord gave her the courage to help people with leprosy and other infectious diseases, putting herself at risk. As she said, "I see Jesus in every human being. I say to myself, this is hungry Jesus; I must feed him. This is sick Jesus. This one has leprosy or gangrene; I must wash him and tend to him. I serve because I love Jesus."

Courageously walk with God and walk lovingly alongside others by adopting these virtues.

1. Affirm others regularly.
2. Be forgiving always.
3. Extend kindness daily.
4. Show gratitude consistently.

## Interpret

God's Word defines what is good and right. He requires us to walk humbly with him and choose to do what is honorable and merciful toward others.

## Apply

How do you characterize your walk with God? What one thing is God calling you to do today that is honorable and demonstrates mercy toward others?

## Pray

*Father, I long to walk closely beside you and to know you more intimately and follow you more faithfully. Help me walk humbly in the direction you desire for my life and give me passion and patience to care for others with mercy and grace.*

# DO UNTO OTHERS

## (PETER'S MOTHER-IN-LAW)

After leaving the synagogue that day, Jesus went to Simon's home, where he found Simon's mother-in-law very sick with a high fever. "Please heal her," everyone begged. Standing at her bedside, he rebuked the fever, and it left her. And she got up at once and prepared a meal for them.

LUKE 4:38–39

## Pray

*Lord, let nothing separate me from you and your Word today. Help me uncover truth and live according to your commands.*

## Observe

How many times growing up did you hear, "Do to others what you would have them do to you?" (Matthew 7:12 NIV). Likely more than you can count. Yet, how often did you sincerely stop to think how your actions impacted the people around you?

Consider this scenario: When chatting with a friend, who is sometimes taken advantage of, she questions why this happens to her. She asks, "Am I doing something wrong? Do they just not care? Or could it be they simply don't realize how their actions make me feel?"

We've all been on both sides of this equation, more often than we likely care to admit. Do you "do to others as you would have them do to you?" God doesn't ask us to be doormats but he does expect us to love—in both actions and words.

We must strive to treat others in ways that honor God and represent our devotion to him.

Only a few verses in the Bible describe Peter's mother-in-law, but it's obvious she loved others well and was deeply loved by many. Luke describes her notoriety in that, "everyone begged" for her to be healed and we clearly see her love displayed by her immediate response in preparing a meal once she was healed.

Courageously do unto others by implementing the following steps.

1. Ask others how you can pray for them and spend time praying over their requests.
2. Let someone know you care by making a call or visit, or by preparing that person a meal.
3. Ask forgiveness from those you've hurt or offended.

4. Look for opportunities to perform
   random acts of kindness.

## Interpret

The ways others speak of us often reveals the ways we've treated or mistreated them. God expects us to express our love for others in both words and action.

## Apply

Think of someone you feel you have mistreated and reach out to that person today with an apology and an act of kindness.

## Pray

*Father, you are the perfect example of love and faithfulness. Through the perfect love of Christ, you extend your mercy and grace. God give me eyes to see clearly how I regard others and help me care for them in ways that honor you.*

## *Day 11*

# REFRAIN FROM JUDGMENT

## (WOMAN WHO ANOINTED JESUS)

One of the Pharisees asked Jesus to have dinner with him, so Jesus went to his home and sat down to eat. When a certain immoral woman from that city heard he was eating there, she brought a beautiful alabaster jar filled with expensive perfume. Then she knelt behind him at his feet, weeping. Her tears fell on his feet, and she wiped them off with her hair. Then she kept kissing his feet and putting perfume on them. Then he turned to the woman and said to Simon, "Look at this woman kneeling here. When I entered your home, you didn't offer me water to wash the dust from my feet, but she has washed them with her tears and wiped them with her hair. You didn't greet me with a kiss, but from the time I first came in, she has not stopped kissing my feet. You neglected the courtesy of olive oil to anoint my head, but she has anointed my feet with rare perfume. I tell you, her sins—and they are many—have been forgiven, so she has shown me much love. But a person who is forgiven little shows only little love."

LUKE 7:36–38, 44–47

*Pray*

*Lord, pierce my heart and challenge my life as I meditate on your Word.*

*Observe*

When we see others sin, we must pause and strive for a Christ-like response.

When considering the sins of others, we are often quick to judge and reluctant to forgive. Yet God's Word teaches us to pursue the opposite. A Christ-like response to sin is seen throughout the Bible and one such example is the beautiful account of Jesus being anointed.

While Jesus was in Bethany dining with Simon, an immoral woman came in and anointed his feet with her tears and perfume. While Simon and the disciples were appalled, Jesus lovingly accepted her expression of adoration and respect. Instead of focusing on her sin, Christ honored her courageous behavior by granting her forgiveness.

Courageously avoid judging others by asking yourself the following questions.

1. Am I willing to be judged in the same way I am judging others (Matthew 7:1–2)?
2. Am I willing to place stumbling blocks in the paths of others (Romans 14:13)?
3. Am I willing to forgive others so I'll be forgiven (Matthew 6:13–15)?
4. Am I willing to show my love for God by being kind and forgiving toward others (Colossians 3:12–13)?

## Interpret

Jesus teaches forgiveness and love, rather than mistreatment and judgment toward sinners.

## Apply

Is there someone you are currently judging? Pray for that person now and determine one way you can encourage him or her today.

## Pray

*Father, help me be kind and tenderhearted toward others. Give me clarity to see past their struggles, wisdom to inspire their recovery, and courage to offer my help.*

# TAKE ACTION

## (CATHERINE BOOTH)

For we are God's masterpiece. He has created us anew in
Christ Jesus, so we can do the good things he planned for us
long ago.

EPHESIANS 2:10

## Pray

*Lord, let me clearly observe truth in your Word and
properly apply it to my life.*

## Observe

Living life empowered with a God-given courage is
a choice—and so is stepping out in faith and following
your God-given commission. Is God challenging you to
embrace courage, step out in faith, and pursue a specific
task? Do you dream of utilizing your gifts and talents,
starting a new career, birthing a ministry, or going on a
mission trip?

When we surrender our lives to Christ, we
begin the process of surrendering our will to God's
purposes and plans. First and foremost, God's plans
for us are to grow closer to him, to learn his Word,

obey his commands, and be a witness for his gospel. But in addition to the everyday ambitions God has for believers, he often calls us individually to embrace specific assignments.

Out of a passionate desire to serve Christ and care for others, Catherine Booth and her husband, William, founded the Salvation Army in 1865. They are remembered for having inspired more than 250,000 men and women to surrender their lives to Christ. At a time when women only played a minimal role in church leadership and had few legal rights, Catherine became a preacher, evangelist, theologian, and co-founder of a ministry that helps to improve the lives of countless people in as many as 128 countries today. Her courageous commitment to lead others to Jesus, along with her legacy of love, sacrifice, and service to others, continues to influence the Salvation Army's mission to this very day.

With God, life can be an adventure—if we just say yes and choose to embrace the courage to launch!

Courageously take action by implementing the following steps.

1. Write out what you believe is your God-given purpose.
2. Pray over what you've written and ask God to reveal his assignment to you.

3. Write a commitment to God stating
   your willingness to say yes.
4. Embrace your God-given courage
   and take action regarding the direction you
   believe God is leading you.

## Interpret

We have been set free and made new through the covering of Christ in order that we might accomplish the purpose and plans God has for our lives.

## Apply

Take one step today to proactively pursue the plans you genuinely believe God is encouraging you to embrace.

## Pray

*Father, you knew me before I was born; you've laid out each day of my life. I will trust you with all of my heart; help me pursue your will all of my days.*

# Day 13
# SEEK HEALING

## (BLEEDING WOMAN)

Just then a woman who had suffered for twelve years with constant bleeding came up behind him. She touched the fringe of his robe, for she thought, "If I can just touch his robe, I will be healed." Jesus turned around, and when he saw her he said, "Daughter, be encouraged! Your faith has made you well." And the woman was healed at that moment.

Matthew 9:20–22

## Pray

*Lord, thank you for the remarkable gift of your Word. Help me to receive your truth.*

## Observe

God wants us to seek healing for ourselves and for others. He tells us in his Word to put our worries aside and pray for everything with a spirit of thanksgiving (Philippians 4:6). He assures us that his peace will guard our hearts and minds no matter what difficulty we face—if we just believe.

God is still in the miracle business, and he wants us to be whole—mind, body, and soul. When we pray for healing, seek his will, and allow him to lead the way, we can rest assured that he will provide the right solution. We may be healed quickly, or we may recover gradually, but one way or another, we will be healed according to his will (Hebrews 2:4).

In today's passage, we meet a woman who was considered unclean and shunned by her people. She risked public humiliation and most likely punishment in order to reach Jesus. She believed in Christ's healing power and courageously trusted him with her life. With just a word from our Savior, she was healed from her bleeding and suffering.

Courageously seek healing by praying this way.

1. Thank God for his many blessings, naming at least five that immediately come to mind.
2. Give God your specific requests for healing—for yourself and for others.
3. Thank God for his healing—past, present, or future—even if it's not in the way you desire.
4. Remain confident in God's promise to heal according to what he knows is best.

## Interpret

God wants us to exercise our faith and come to him for healing, and he will heal us according to his will in his perfect timing.

## Apply

Are you or someone you know in need of healing? Go before God's throne of grace today and ask him for a miraculous healing according to his will.

## Pray

*Father, I'm coming to you today as your child, longing to hear from you and asking for your divine healing. There's so much I don't understand about life. But I do know that with one touch, one word, you can make me whole.*

# BE WILLING TO SERVE

## (WOMEN WHO WORKED ALONGSIDE PAUL)

Indeed, true companion, I ask you also to help these women
who have shared my struggle in *the cause of* the gospel,
together with Clement also and the rest of my fellow workers,
whose names are in the book of life.

PHILIPPIANS 4:3 NASB

## Pray

*Lord, give me a deeper understanding of you and
your Word.*

## Observe

Scripture tells us that God gives each of us specific
gifts and talents we are to use in service to one another
(1 Peter 4:10). We don't earn these gifts; they are an
expression of God's love. And we don't choose our gifts;
they are determined by God, given to us by the Holy
Spirit, to equip us for service, in order to build up the
body of Christ (1 Corinthians 12:11; Ephesians 4:12).

In today's "all about me" culture, being a servant
isn't an attribute many people strive for. It's not a
popular concept, it doesn't come with a glamorous title,

and our friends and co-workers aren't likely to challenge us for the position. However, it reveals the heart of our character and the root of our priorities. And it is an attribute God generously blesses us for, as he blesses others through us.

In Philippians 4:3, the apostle Paul commends women who have labored alongside him for the sake of the gospel. And he calls on Philippians to help these courageous women in honor of their work.

Jesus did not come to be served, but to serve, and to give his life for you and me (Matthew 20:28). The least we can do is follow his lead and be courageously willing to serve others for the sake of his kingdom.

Be courageously willing to serve others by following these steps.

1. Identify genuine needs within your family, workplace, community, and/or local church.
2. Pray over each need and ask God to reveal the one or ones he wants you to meet.
3. Determine the necessary steps you can take to help meet the need God has asked you to address.
4. Take action and remain committed to the task until the need has been met or God brings in other workers.

## Interpret

We are to be fellow workers in God's kingdom, in the same way the women of Paul's time were.

## Apply

Ask God to reveal your specific area of kingdom work and dedicate yourself to that work, even when it's difficult.

## Pray

*Father, give me wisdom and discernment to know where and how you desire for me to contribute to your kingdom work. Prepare me for service and help me succeed.*

# DARE TO DREAM

## (CLARA BARTON)

So we keep on praying for you, asking our God to enable you to live a life worthy of his call. May he give you the power to accomplish all the good things your faith prompts you to do.

2 Thessalonians 1:11

## *Pray*

*Lord, teach me from your Word and help me walk in your ways.*

## *Observe*

When was the last time you dreamed?

Dreaming focuses on the future, it sees beyond our current circumstances into the possibilities of what could be. We develop various dreams and ambitions throughout our lives; some are godly, while others are more worldly and self-focused. Dreams are an integral part of the direction our lives take. Therefore we must evaluate them carefully, and then pursue honorable ones passionately.

God has God-sized dreams for us if we are willing to move beyond where we are. If we set aside time with the Lord, he will reveal the direction he wants to take us. God's dreams are far beyond what we can think or imagine, and he will open the doors to our dreams if we will submit to his plans and allow him to lead.

At a young age, Clara Barton dreamed of caring for the needy. Through a passionate desire to nurse wounded animals and injured pets, she prepared for a life that would be dedicated to serving men, women, and families who were in desperate need. During the Civil War, Clara risked her life to bring needed supplies to soldiers who were out in the field. She was intelligent, strong-willed, and determined. At sixty years of age, she founded the American Red Cross and led it for the next twenty-three years. Today, Clara Barton is one of the most honored women in American history.

Courageously dare to dream by exercising these following steps.

1. Write your dreams down on a piece of paper and pray over them.
2. Ask yourself: *Do I believe these dreams are ones that God desires for me?*
3. Ask God for wisdom, discernment, and to reveal his dreams for your future.
4. Seek wise counsel, set measurable goals, and begin following your dreams!

## Interpret

God will give us the power to accomplish the things our faith prompts us to do so that we might live a life worthy of his calling.

## Apply

What dream has God placed on your heart? Take the first step today toward realizing your dream by sharing it with a godly friend and ask him or her to pray for you.

## Pray

*Father, thank you for giving me dreams and for promising to be with me as I strive to achieve those dreams. Please help me discern your will and give me the courage to choose rightly as I consider my choices.*

# STEP OUT OF YOUR COMFORT ZONE

## (THE WISE WOMAN OF TEKOA)

And King David, now reconciled to Amnon's death, longed to be reunited with his son Absalom. Joab realized how much the king longed to see Absalom. So he sent for a woman from Tekoa who had a reputation for great wisdom. He said to her, "Pretend you are in mourning; wear mourning clothes and don't put on lotions. Act like a woman who has been mourning for the dead for a long time. Then go to the king and tell him the story I am about to tell you." Then Joab told her what to say. When the woman from Tekoa approached the king, she bowed with her face to the ground in deep respect and cried out, "O king! Help me!"

2 Samuel 13:39–14:4

## Pray

*Lord, please give me wisdom as I approach your Word.*

## Observe

When we consider our God-given dreams, our natural courage and strength are often quickly replaced with fear. But God never leaves us after giving us a dream. He always equips us with everything we need to accomplish his will.

God often asks us to do things we're unqualified for and unprepared to do. Pursuing God's calling typically stretches our faith and can be downright uncomfortable. Fear can usher in doubt and keep us from moving forward. But we don't have to embrace our fears. God is ready to help—if we will simply say yes, embrace his courage, and take the first step.

King David missed his son Absalom terribly but was unwilling to forgive him. So David's commander, Joab, devised a plan and called on a wise woman from Tekoa to help him execute it. When the woman approached David, she recited her story and revealed her true intention. As a result of her faith and her willingness to step courageously outside her comfort zone, David agreed to bring Absalom home, and the two were reunited.

Courageously step out your comfort zone by asking yourself the following questions.

1. What hopes and dreams has God placed on my heart?
2. What gifts and talents has God given me?
3. What steps can I take to pursue God's calling?
4. Who can I call that will encourage and support me as I step outside my comfort zone?

### Interpret

God blesses us and restores our lives when we step out of our comfort zone and pursue his calling.

### Apply

What is God encouraging you to do today? Determine your first step, embrace your God-given courage, and take action.

### Pray

*Father, reveal to me the plans and purposes you have for my life. Help me know what to do to pursue your will and give me supernatural courage to take the first step.*

# COMMUNICATE WITH CARE

## (EUODIA AND SYNTYCHE)

Now I appeal to Euodia and Syntyche. Please, because you
belong to the Lord, settle your disagreement. And I ask you,
my true partner, to help these two women, for they worked
hard with me in telling others the Good News. They worked
along with Clement and the rest of my co-workers, whose
names are written in the Book of Life.

PHILIPPIANS 4:2–3

### Pray

*Lord, give me focus and direction as I study your*
*Word.*

### Observe

Better communication leads to better relationships.

God calls us to speak truth, and He calls us to do
so in love (Ephesians 4:15). In order to communicate
with care, we must avoid responses that kill our
conversations. Four conversation killers are criticism,
defensiveness, stonewalling, and contempt.

Criticism is often used when we disagree,
disapprove, object, or judge other people's thoughts

or actions. Defensiveness is often employed when someone disagrees, disapproves, objects, or judges us. Criticism and defensiveness place our conversations into a destructive, repetitive cycle—a cycle that repeats itself until one person gives up, shuts down, or walks away.

Contempt is an expression of disgust or dislike, and stonewalling is a refusal to communicate. Knowing how destructive these conversation killers are doesn't stop us from employing them. We must make every effort to communicate with patience, compassion, and a willingness to listen—whether we agree with what is being said or not.

Euodia and Syntyche partnered with Paul in the spread of the gospel, and he urged them to communicate with care. These sisters in Christ were encouraged to settle their disagreement and focus on their calling to influence the world for Christ.

Courageously communicate with care by regularly asking yourself the following questions.

1. Is God encouraging me to reconcile with someone with whom I am at odds?
2. Am I quick to judge and criticize people for their faults?
3. Has someone judged or criticized me, and does their judgment have any merit?

4. Am I willing to thank others for their honest evaluations? Do I need to ask someone for forgiveness, or do I need to set a healthy boundary in order to guard my heart?

## Interpret

God wants us to be at peace with others and maintain our focus on spreading the gospel.

## Apply

Practice courageous communication by reaching out today to someone who has criticized you. Thank that person for his or her honest opinion and ask that individual to pray for you as you strive to change.

## Pray

*Father, help me to be quick to hear, slow to speak, and slow to anger (James 1:19). Give me the courage to communicate truth in love and help me to do all I can do to be at peace with everyone (Romans 12:18).*

# Day 18
# LET GOD LEAD

## (TAMMIE JO SHULTS)

Don't be afraid, for I am with you. Don't be discouraged,
for I am your God. I will strengthen you and help you.
I will hold you up with my victorious right hand.

ISAIAH 41:10

## Pray

*Lord, let your Word give me guidance and direction.*

## Observe

We often face life in our own strength and allow
our fears to overwhelm us in the midst of a challenge or
crisis. The best way to quiet our concerns is to willfully
embrace our God-given courage and trust him to lead.
God, according to his mighty power at work within us,
can accomplish far more than we might ever ask or
dream (Ephesians 3:20).

The Lord doesn't intend for us to face our
challenges alone. He designed us to rely on him and
live in community with others where help and support
are readily available. Therefore, we must let go and let
God lead.

Once we acknowledge the challenges that keep us trapped in fear, we can begin implementing daily practices that help us overcome our apprehension in order to embrace our God-given opportunities. We must always remember that Christ calls us to lay aside our hindrances and pursue his will by keeping our eyes on him, the one who perfects our faith, gives us courage, and sees us through (Hebrews 12:1–2).

Tammie Jo Shults successfully landed Southwest Airlines Flight 1380 on April 17, 2018 after one of its engines exploded. Seven passengers were injured and one died when shrapnel from the engine blew out one of the plane's windows. Tammie, one of the first female combat aviators in the United States Navy, successfully made the emergency landing, avoiding a much greater tragedy and saving the lives of 144 passengers. As soon as the plane landed, Tammie quickly gave credit to God. Tammie's close friends credit her with a "deep Christian faith" and "a fierce determination and laser focus" that accompany her sweetness.

Courageously let God lead by adopting the following practices.

1. Acknowledge your fears and pray daily for courage.
2. Reach out to godly friends or loved ones and ask them to pray.

3. Keep your eyes on Christ, his presence, his hope, and his help.
4. Completely trust God with the outcome of your situations and circumstances.

## Interpret

Fear is a tactic of satan, but God gives us power, love, and discipline in all life situations.

## Apply

What fears are currently causing you anxiety and apprehension? Ask God to settle your spirit and help you move forward in courage today.

## Pray

*Father, thank you for leading me by your spirit and comforting me when I'm afraid. Please help me be strong and courageous as I face intimidating life experiences.*

# GRASP THE TRUTH

## (THE WISE WOMAN OF ABEL-BETH-MAACAH)

When Joab's forces arrived, they attacked Abel-beth-maacah.
They built a siege ramp against the town's fortifications and
began battering down the wall. But a wise woman in the town
called out to Joab, "Listen to me, Joab. Come over here so I
can talk to you." … "I am one who is peace loving and faithful
in Israel. But you are destroying an important town in Israel.
Why do you want to devour what belongs to the LORD?"

2 SAMUEL 20:15–16, 19

*Pray*

*Lord, let your Word be a mirror into my soul.*

*Observe*

Satan is the master of lies and he desires to
deceive, distract, and destroy us at every turn.
Throughout our lives, we can find ourselves lured
into false beliefs as a result of misinformation from
loved ones, friends, and well-meaning teachers. It's
even possible to be exposed to false doctrines and
misunderstandings of God's Word. After all, satan loves
to tempt us to question it, just as he did to Eve. Exposure
to these types of distortions can lead us into making

poor choices. We sometimes even base life's most important decisions around our misguided beliefs.

In 2 Samuel chapter 20, Joab, the commander of King David's army, was prepared to attack and destroy the entire city of Abel-beth-maacah. As they prepared for battle, a brave, wise woman approached Joab and urged him not to destroy Abel-beth-maacah, an important city that belonged to God. As a result of her courage to confront Joab with the truth and his willingness to embrace that truth, the city was spared.

It's critically important throughout our lives that we identify and eliminate any distorted and worldly beliefs we've adopted and learn to live in the light of God's truth as he reveals it to us in his Word.

Courageously embrace God's truth by implementing the following practices.

1. Approach God's Word inductively by putting your beliefs aside and allowing God's Word to unveil the truth.
2. Study God's Word faithfully by implementing practical Bible study steps for proper interpretation.
3. Memorize verses of Scripture to secure God's truth in your heart and mind.

4. As you read, study, and memorize God's Word, be mindful to identify worldly lies that you've believed and replace those lies with God's unchanging truth.

## Interpret

God never wants us to base our choices on misinformation. Embracing truth enables wise decisions, and we prosper as a result.

## Apply

Can you name one worldly lie you used to believe, and the truth from God's Word that eliminated that lie?

## Pray

*Father, give me wisdom to recognize any worldly lies I've adopted and help me replace the lies with truth from your Word.*

# CHOOSE COURAGE

## (DEBORAH)

"Very well," she replied, "I will go with you. But you will receive no honor in this venture, for the LORD's victory over Sisera will be at the hands of a woman." So Deborah went with Barak to Kedesh. At Kedesh, Barak called together the tribes of Zebulun and Naphtali, and 10,000 warriors went up with him. Deborah also went with him.

JUDGES 4:9–10

*Pray*

*Lord, give me the ability to see the wondrous truth in your Word.*

*Observe*

How can we maintain courage even when life gets difficult?

Courage is an attribute of integrity that gives us strength to make better decisions in the midst of fearful and difficult situations. We all need courage for something. Depending on our circumstances, there are different types of courage we need, ranging from physical strength and endurance, to mental stamina and innovation. My favorite definition of courage is "taking a risk and trusting God with the outcome."

The first step in any new direction is always the hardest. Maybe you need to submit your application for a new job, schedule an appointment with a Christian counselor, or agree to forgive someone who has wounded your heart. No matter what God is encouraging you to do, don't let the fear keep you from experiencing the joy and freedom God is calling you to embrace.

God wants us to face life with courage, hope, and unwavering faith. The Bible offers numerous accounts of courageous women and men whose lives inspire us to make better choices and live more courageously. Take for example Deborah. Deborah was a wife, prophetess, ruler, and warrior. She was the fifth Judge over Israel, appointed by God to lead the people out of bondage. Deborah courageously led her army into battle against an enemy who outnumbered them ten-to-one. She exercised great courage, maintained confidence in God's deliverance, and was known throughout the land as the female leader and warrior who rescued Israel.

Courageously choose courage by implementing the following steps.

1. Seek and embrace godly counsel.
2. Fast and pray, asking God for courage and guidance.

3. Place your confidence in God's plan and take action, even if you're afraid.
4. Trust God with your outcome.

### Interpret

God allows us to experience life situations that require unwavering faith and God-given courage. If we rely on him, he will lead us into victory.

### Apply

What courageous action or change is God calling you to make? Set aside your fear, embrace your God-given courage, and take your first step today.

### Pray

*Father, show me the changes you want me to make and the direction you want me to go. Give me courage to take action and endurance to see it through.*

*Day 21*

# CHANGE DIRECTION

### (LINDA FULLER)

*Therefore, since we are surrounded by such a huge crowd of witnesses to the life of faith, let us strip off every weight that slows us down, especially the sin that so easily trips us up. And let us run with endurance the race God has set before us.*

HEBREWS 12:1

## Pray

Lord, let nothing separate me from you and your Word today. Help me uncover truth and live according to your commands.

## Observe

In today's busy culture, we always seem to be running. Running here and there—trying to keep up with family, friends, projects, responsibilities, and upcoming events. In the midst of our busy schedules, it's vital we ask ourselves: *Which way am I running and which way does God want me to run?*

Each day, we find ourselves running toward people and things and away from people and things. How often do you stop to think about what or whom you are running *toward*, or what or whom you are running *from*?

God has prepared opportunities and adventures for us. Yet past sin, pain, and failure often cause us to hesitate when God prompts us to make a change in direction. It's up to us to recognize the possibilities, set aside our obstacles, and courageously walk toward God's will.

Linda Fuller and her husband, Millard, founded Habitat for Humanity International in 1976. Success and wealth brought their marriage to a breaking point. Rather than accepting things as they were, they re-evaluated their lives and decided to make a drastic life change. They sold their possessions and dedicated the rest of their lives to Christian service, "seeking to put God's love into action." Today, "more than 13.2 million people have built or improved a stronger, more stable place to live with the organization's help."

Courageously change the direction of your life by applying the following principles.

1. Prayerfully evaluate the direction your life is currently heading.
2. Prayerfully consider the direction you believe God wants you to go.
3. Seek godly counsel regarding the process of change.
4. Determine the necessary steps and begin taking action.

## Interpret

God has a plan for our lives. It's up to us to remove the obstacles that stand in our way and follow his direction with endurance and determination.

## Apply

Do you sense God calling you to change the direction of your life? Reach out to a godly friend, loved one, or mentor today and ask him or her to help you evaluate the path you believe God is encouraging you to take.

## Pray

*Father, thank you for preparing the way I should go. Please help me run toward you and in the direction of your will, even if it means I have to completely change directions.*

# KEEP A HOPE-FILLED FOCUS

## (RAHAB)

Before the spies went to sleep that night, Rahab went up on the roof to talk with them. "I know the LORD has given you this land," she told them. "We are all afraid of you. Everyone in the land is living in terror. For we have heard how the LORD made a dry path for you through the Red Sea when you left Egypt." … For the LORD your God is the supreme God of the heavens above and the earth below.

JOSHUA 2:8–10; 11

## Pray

*Lord, teach me from your Word and help me walk in your ways.*

## Observe

How often do you consciously consider your focus?

We're each given the opportunity to choose either a positive or negative perspective toward each situation we face. We're all given the free will to pursue God's will and ways—or our own dreams and desires.

In the second chapter of Joshua, we meet a courageous woman named Rahab—a woman who is recognized in the Book of Hebrews as a woman of great faith (11:31). Rahab was a woman with a shameful past (Joshua 2:1) who could've hidden in fear or betrayed Joshua's men. Yet she believed in God, chose obedience to him, protected the Israelites, and is included in the lineage of Christ; she became the great-great-grandmother of King David (Matthew 1:5).

In learning to keep a hope-filled focus, it is critical we keep our eyes on Christ. Unless we trust God completely and pursue his will and ways faithfully, we will be forever vulnerable to our inner-accuser who anxiously waits to bury us in fear. When we direct our attention toward God, he gives us courage and confidence for our life journeys.

Keep a hope-filled courage by adopting the following practices.

1. Be faithful in your daily prayer life.
2. Each day, think of ten things you're thankful for and make them your focus.
3. Memorize Bible verses that encourage you.
4. Seek godly counsel for inspiration, wisdom, and guidance.

## Interpret

Rahab fixed her eyes on loyalty to the one true God. We are strong and courageous when we fix our eyes on Christ and make him the focus of our decisions and directions.

## Apply

Set your mind on the things above, not on the things of this world (Colossians 3:2) by memorizing Scripture. Take a significant step today by asking God to reveal his will for your life and take at least one significant step toward obeying God's calling.

## Pray

*Father, help me to tune out the inner voices that keep me steeped in fear and selfishness. Allow me to see life through your lens, where my hope is restored and your help is always near.*

# FACE YOUR FEARS

## (MARY, MOTHER OF JESUS)

This is how Jesus the Messiah was born. His mother, Mary, was engaged to be married to Joseph. But before the marriage took place, while she was still a virgin, she became pregnant through the power of the Holy Spirit. Joseph, to whom she was engaged, was a righteous man and did not want to disgrace her publicly, so he decided to break the engagement quietly.

MATTHEW 1:18–19

## Pray

*Lord, let your Word be a light unto my path.*

## Observe

Fear can be a catalyst for stress and anxiety. It can be the adhesive that keeps our issues firmly attached, hindering our ability to heal.

When God created us, he created us with an awareness of our surroundings, with the ability to discern good from evil, safety from danger, and right from wrong. Healthy fears function as an internal alarm system. When we approach unsafe situations or consider making poor decisions, we are warned of potential danger.

Unhealthy fears, on the other hand, can paralyze us and keep us from making wise decisions. These fears overwhelm our emotions, foster irrational thoughts, and often keep us from experiencing the abundant life Christ wants for us.

The fear of man causes us to walk a path of deception and leads us into sin and away from God. The fear of God gives us wisdom and inspires us to turn away from sin and trust God.

Mary, the mother of Jesus, chose to face her fears the night the angel Gabriel appeared to her to announce she would deliver the Messiah. Mary was young, a virgin, and engaged to be married. Without a rock-solid faith in God and a determination to persevere through her circumstances, Mary likely would have crumbled in fear when she learned she would supernaturally conceive a child. But Scripture reveals she immediately yielded her life to God's will saying, "I am the Lord's servant. May everything you have said about me come true" (Luke 1:38).

Courageously face your fears by implementing the following steps.

1. Seek comfort in God's presence (Psalm 23:4).
2. Cling to scriptural truth (John 17:17).
3. Consult godly counsel (Proverbs 12:15).
4. Trust God with the outcome (Jeremiah 29:11).

## Interpret

Although God allows us to go through life experiences that are fearful, he calls us to face our fears by fully trusting him with our circumstances and future.

## Apply

Are you currently facing a fearful situation? Decide today to give your fears to God, ask him for guidance, and make a commitment to fully trust him with your direction and outcome.

## Pray

*Father, you know my circumstances and the path that's best for me to walk through this life journey. Give me unwavering courage to face my fears and allow me to completely trust you every step of the way.*

# PRAY WITH CONFIDENCE

## (AMY CARMICHAEL)

Are any of you suffering hardships? You should pray. Are any of you happy? You should sing praises. Are any of you sick? You should call for the elders of the church to come and pray over you, anointing you with oil in the name of the Lord. Such a prayer offered in faith will heal the sick, and the Lord will make you well. And if you have committed any sins, you will be forgiven. Confess your sins to each other and pray for each other so that you may be healed. The earnest prayer of a righteous person has great power and produces wonderful results.

JAMES 5:13–16

*Pray*

*Lord, pierce my heart and challenge my life as I meditate on your Word.*

*Observe*

Our prayers are to consist of heartfelt thoughts and verbal pleas we share with God. We are to rally family and friends to join us in praying. We are to pray for our leaders, even those we don't agree with. We are to pray at all times and in all places. We can pray while driving, pray while exercising, and even pray in the midst of a completely consuming project. We are to pray again and again when, out of the blue, God brings a person, place, or need to our mind.

Irish missionary, Amy Carmichael, sailed to India and was extremely distressed when she learned of the countless children who were being forced into ritual prostitution. Shortly thereafter, Amy founded the Dohnavur Fellowship that rescued hundreds of children from this horrific fate. Called "Amma," meaning mother, by the children, she made great use of her brown eyes and used tea bags to dye her skin, in order to be permitted into Hindu temples where she would rescue children. Amy's ministry success has been credited to her faithful dedication to Scripture and prayer.

Consider the following promises from God and learn to courageously pray with confidence.

1. God promises to hear our prayers (Jeremiah 29:12).
2. God promises to be near when we pray (Psalm 145:18).
3. God promises the Holy Spirit will help and intercede as we pray (Romans 8:26).
4. God promises to answer our prayers (John 15:7).

## Interpret

God wants his followers to pray at all times, over all things; for there is great power in prayer as God hears and answers our prayers.

## Apply

Ask God to place one person on your heart that needs prayer and make time today to repeatedly lift up his or her name and needs to our Father in heaven.

## Pray

*Father, thank you for hearing and responding to my prayers. Help me remain confident as I pray, knowing you will answer my prayers in the way that is best.*

# WATCH YOUR WORDS

### (MARTHA)

Martha was distracted by the big dinner she was preparing. She came to Jesus and said, "Lord, doesn't it seem unfair to you that my sister just sits here while I do all the work? Tell her to come and help me." But the Lord said to her, "My dear Martha, you are worried and upset over all these details! There is only one thing worth being concerned about. Mary has discovered it, and it will not be taken away from her."

LUKE 10:40–42

### Pray

Lord, unlock the mysteries of your Word that I might know your will.

### Observe

Words can be helpful or harmful, and it's critical to our spiritual, emotional, and relational health that we engage in regular checkups to assess how our words are impacting others and how their words are affecting us. Toxic words become lies, which can lead to distraction, inaction, and even depression.

If we take in hurtful words and allow them to define and defeat us, we will find it difficult, if not impossible, to accomplish God's will in our lives. If we have a habit of criticizing and complaining about others, we will plant seeds of doubt and negativity that can cause others to doubt their abilities, become discouraged, and give up on their God-given dreams.

The more time we spend focusing on what others are doing or not doing, the less time we have to focus on things that really matter—like time spent with Christ.

Mary's sister, Martha, allowed her emotions to influence her actions. She was so upset with her sister that she felt it necessary to complain to Jesus. Martha became so preoccupied with what she believed was important, that she fell prey to judgment and criticism and missed a God-given opportunity to sit at the feet of Christ.

Courageously watch your words by asking yourself the following questions.

1. Do you respond to pain or disappointment by attacking others with hurtful words?
2. Do you allow verbal attacks from others to distract, discourage, or defeat you?
3. Will you set healthy boundaries with people who are verbally attacking you?
4. Will you strive to speak words that will build yourself and others up rather than tearing them down?

## Interpret

Jesus wants us to refrain from complaints and criticism and place our focus on things that really matter, like spending time with him.

## Apply

Have you been hurtful to someone with your words? Reach out to them today, ask for forgiveness, and make a commitment to change your words.

## Pray

*Father, help me avoid words that offend and use words that edify others so I can be an instrument of your grace.*

# BE A GODLY INFLUENCE

## (MONAOH'S WIFE)

As the flames from the altar shot up toward the sky, the angel of the LORD ascended in the fire. When Manoah and his wife saw this, they fell with their faces to the ground. The angel did not appear again to Manoah and his wife. Manoah finally realized it was the angel of the LORD, and he said to his wife, "We will certainly die, for we have seen God!" But his wife said, "If the LORD were going to kill us, he wouldn't have accepted our burnt offering and grain offering. He wouldn't have appeared to us and told us this wonderful thing and done these miracles." When her son was born, she named him Samson. And the LORD blessed him as he grew up.

JUDGES 13:20–24

## Pray

*Lord, help me develop a deeper desire for you as I encounter your Word.*

## Observe

You don't have to speak to large audiences, write a book, own a thriving business, or have a big social media following to have influence. More often than not, influence happens around our everyday, ordinary events of life—around the dinner table, in a living room, at a coffee shop, or during a small group discussion. In fact, whether we realize it or not, we influence family members, neighbors, co-workers, and friends all the time by our words, actions, and choices.

God doesn't give us our insights, gifts, and talents just for our own personal gain. He is much more concerned with how we use these qualities to serve him and bless others (Colossians 3:23; 1 Peter 4:10).

In the book of Judges, chapter 13, Samson's father, Monoah, was terrified that God was going to kill him and his wife. But Monoah's courageous wife gently encouraged her husband with her knowledge of God and unwavering faith.

Courageously influence others in godly ways by eliminating the following obstacles.

1. Don't allow your past to discourage you from being a positive influence.
2. Don't allow your weaknesses to distract you from being a faithful encourager.
3. Don't allow the opinions of others to keep you from being an inspiration.
4. Don't allow fear to stop you from sharing your faith and leading others to Christ.

## Interpret

When other people misunderstand God, his Word, and his ways, God wants us to courageously express our faith and gently lead them to the truth.

## Apply

Who do you influence? Evaluate the ways in which you influence others and determine if it's in alignment with God and his Word.

## Pray

*Father, you give me everything I need to faithfully lead others. Prepare my heart and mind to be a godly influence and give me unshakable courage to lead others to you.*

# EMBRACE YOUR CIRCUMSTANCES

### (JONI EARECKSON TADA)

We can rejoice, too, when we run into problems and trials, for we know that they help us develop endurance. And endurance develops strength of character, and character strengthens our confident hope of salvation. And this hope will not lead to disappointment. For we know how dearly God loves us, because he has given us the Holy Spirit to fill our hearts with his love.

ROMANS 5:3–5

## Pray

*Lord, please give me wisdom as I approach your Word and learn from your precepts.*

## Observe

When events in our lives are more positive, we tend to be happy and have a more optimistic outlook. When our circumstances are more challenging, we tend to be unhappy and adopt a negative perspective on life.

When we experience times of hopelessness, brokenness, and despair, it can be hard to muster up the strength to keep going. But through our trials, we learn to keep our eyes on Christ, the author and perfecter of our faith and future. Therefore we must strive to focus on the things we can be thankful for and choose a positive outlook, no matter the situation or struggle.

Joni Eareckson Tada became paralyzed and confined to a wheelchair as a result of a diving accident in 1967. After several years of rehabilitation, she embraced her circumstances and was determined to help others with similar disabilities. Since that time, she has authored over fifty books and is a well-known artist, columnist, and speaker. Joni openly shares how she initially struggled to accept God's new plan for her life and describes her courageous outlook in this way, "For a wheelchair may confine a body that is wasting away. But no wheelchair can confine the soul … the soul that is inwardly renewed day by day."

Courageously embrace your circumstances by adopting the following practices.

1. Focus on the eternal over the temporary (2 Corinthians 4:18).
2. Remain positive, trusting God to work all things together for good (Romans 8:28).
3. Devote yourself to prayer with an attitude of thanksgiving (Colossians 4:2).
4. Place your hope in God's ability to take care of your future (Jeremiah 29:11).

## Interpret

God wants us to embrace hope and joy in the midst of our suffering, and he wants to strengthen our character and our ability to endure as we go through life's trials.

## Apply

Make a commitment today to adopt a positive outlook and attitude toward your circumstances and let others see your new perspective through your actions and behaviors.

## Pray

*Father, I am grateful you use everything I go through to help me become a better person. Please give me the ability to see past my pain and the courage to endure my trials.*

# KEEP THE FAITH

## (HANNAH)

There was a man named Elkanah who lived in Ramah in the region of Zuph in the hill country of Ephraim. He was the son of Jeroham, son of Elihu, son of Tohu, son of Zuph, of Ephraim. Elkanah had two wives, Hannah and Peninnah. Peninnah had children, but Hannah did not. … So Peninnah would taunt Hannah and make fun of her because the LORD had kept her from having children. … Once after a sacrificial meal at Shiloh, Hannah got up and went to pray. Eli the priest was sitting at his customary place beside the entrance of the Tabernacle. Hannah was in deep anguish, crying bitterly as she prayed to the Lord.

1 SAMUEL 1:1–2, 6, 9–10

## Pray

*Lord, please give me wisdom as I approach your Word and learn from your precepts.*

## Observe

If you were building a house, you would never start framing until a solid foundation was properly in place. So why not approach your spiritual life with the same care and concern? Without a strong foundation, our houses crumble in severe storms. Similarly, without a solid spiritual foundation, we crumble—sometimes at the mere mention of a storm.

To construct a solid spiritual foundation, we must *hear, understand,* and *act on* the teachings of Christ. Jesus makes it clear that throughout life we will encounter painful life storms (John 16:33). He also makes it clear that if we *hear his words* and *don't act on them,* we're in store for a great fall (Matthew 7:26–27).

Hannah devoted her life to following God. She consistently prayed and faithfully trusted God with her future. Because of Hannah's firm foundation of faith, she endured the cruel treatment by Peninnah, and Hannah's prayers were answered when God gave her a son, the great prophet Samuel.

Courageously strengthen your spiritual foundation by implementing the following practices.

1. Set aside time each day for quiet prayer.
2. Read the Bible at least four or more times each week. Consider reading through the book of James chapter by chapter.
3. Consider joining a Bible study and challeng yourself to consistently read, study, and apply God's truth to your life.
4. Consider reaching out to a mature Christian friend and ask that individual to disciple you.

## Interpret

Believers can weather any hardship or cruel treatment when their faith is firm, and they trust God with their future.

## Apply

How strong is your spiritual foundation? What step will you take today to strengthen your faith?

## Pray

*Father, give me wisdom as I seek to strengthen my faith and help me build a strong foundation in you to weather the storms of life that seek to distract, discourage, and destroy me.*

# SEEK COURAGE

## (MARY, MARK'S MOTHER)

When he realized this, he went to the home of Mary, the mother of John Mark, where many were gathered for prayer. He knocked at the door in the gate, and a servant girl named Rhoda came to open it. When she recognized Peter's voice, she was so overjoyed that, instead of opening the door, she ran back inside and told everyone, "Peter is standing at the door!" "You're out of your mind!" they said. When she insisted, they decided, "It must be his angel." Meanwhile, Peter continued knocking. When they finally opened the door and saw him, they were amazed. He motioned for them to quiet down and told them how the Lord had led him out of prison.

ACTS 12:12–17

*Pray*

*Lord, help me to hunger and thirst for your promises found in your Word.*

*Observe*

Courage is the ability to confront fear with unwavering faith and to face conflicts, difficult tasks, illnesses, and loss with strength. Courage is also our willingness to say and do what's right, regardless of popularity or profitability.

We all need courage, but we don't naturally possess it—we must intentionally seek it. Too often, we instinctively strive to protect and nurture our own self-interests. Embracing what is *right* over what is *safe* can be a daunting challenge. But we don't have to face our fears alone.

The greatest source of true courage is found in Jesus Christ. When we recognize Christ as our provider of courage, he can give us the power to make wise decisions, regardless of the consequences. He can deliver us from our fears and give us the courage to take on new challenges, confront conflicts, pursue career changes, and face illnesses, losses, and a multitude of other adversities with unwavering faith.

Mary, the mother of Mark, embraced faith-filled courage and offered her home as a place of prayer and refuge for believers during a time of severe persecution.

Courageously seek courage from God by implementing the following four steps.

1. Acknowledge God's presence and his promise to be with you at all times.
2. Pray God's Word and stand firm in his assurances.
3. Trust God completely with his plan for your life.

4. Wait for God's timing, being
   confident he knows best.

## Interpret

God wants us to stand firm in our faith and exercise our God-given courage at all times, even when facing persecution.

## Apply

Is God calling you to stand firm in your faith? Exercise your courage muscles today and share your faith with a stranger and offer to pray for them.

## Pray

*Father, thank you for your presence and promises. Help me stand firm in my faith and give me courage to pursue your will and your ways.*

# Day 30
# CHOOSE TO LOVE
## (CORRIE TEN BOOM)

Love is patient and kind. Love is not jealous or boastful or proud or rude. It does not demand its own way. It is not irritable, and it keeps no record of being wronged. It does not rejoice about injustice but rejoices whenever the truth wins out. Love never gives up, never loses faith, is always hopeful, and endures through every circumstance.

1 Corinthians 13:4–7

## Pray

*Lord, give me a deeper understanding of you and your Word.*

## Observe

Love is an attitude of the heart—it's choosing to love in spite of faults and failures, hurts and hardships. It's standing by someone's side to help that person navigate the ups and downs of life in spite of his or her actions or attitude. It's getting past hurtful words, actions, and behaviors. It's realizing we are all human, fallible, and totally capable of (and likely to) hurt one another, let one another down, and break one another's heart. Love is tested by time, patience, and endurance.

In Corrie ten Boom's famous book, *The Hiding Place*, she describes how she and her family protected many Jews from the Nazi Holocaust during World War II. Corrie and her sister were arrested, along with many other family members, and sent to a woman's labor camp, where she narrowly escaped death. She considered her life a gift from God and shared with the world the truth she and her sister learned from their experiences: "So I discovered that it is not on our forgiveness any more than on our goodness that the world's healing hinges, but on His. When He tells us to love our enemies, He gives, along with the command, the love itself." Having truly grasped God's never-ending love, Corrie ten Boom made it her life's pursuit to travel the world teaching others about God's unconditional love and forgiveness.

Courageously choose to love by exercising the following principles.

1. Determine to love in spite of circumstances, situations, or responses from others.
2. Take into consideration the difficulties and challenges others might be facing.
3. Set aside bitterness and unforgiveness and replace them with understanding and love.

4. Search for ways to outwardly and intentionally show unconditional love toward others.

## Interpret

Love is the never-ending ability to see past the faults of others, and God commands his followers to love in the same way he graciously loves us.

## Apply

Do you truly grasp God's love for you, and are you willing to share that love with others, even those who have offended you? Ask God to bring one person to mind and share God's love with that individual today.

## Pray

*Father, thank you for unconditionally and always loving me in spite of my faults and failures. Help me forgive those who have wounded me; show them the same love you so mercifully show me.*

## Day 31

# PURSUE KNOWLEDGE

### (MARY, MARTHA'S SISTER)

As Jesus and the disciples continued on their way to Jerusalem, they came to a certain village where a woman named Martha welcomed him into her home. Her sister, Mary, sat at the Lord's feet, listening to what he taught. But Martha was distracted by the big dinner she was preparing.

Luke 10:38–40

## Pray

*Lord, give me wisdom and understanding of you and your precepts as I study your Word.*

## Observe

Knowledge is something we acquire throughout life. Some like to learn by studying, researching, and reading books, while others prefer to learn hands on. We inevitably gain some knowledge day to day as we experience life, but knowledge is more than something simply "to be gained through life experiences." It is a gift, something we should embrace and zealously pursue; and as Christians, it is a vital part of our spiritual maturity (2 Peter 1:5–6, 3:18).

When we study the word *knowledge* in Scripture, we find its root word, *yāda'*, (which means "to know"), occurs 944 times in the Bible. I've heard it said that true knowledge is experiential. Experiential knowledge is gained when we apply what we've learned to our lives. We acquire a much deeper understanding of what we've learned when we invest time practicing our newly acquired skill or principle. So it's not only important that we consistently engage in *learning* but also consistently engage in *applying* what we've learned to our everyday lives.

Jesus praised Mary for doing the "one thing worth being concerned about," sitting at his feet, taking in his teaching (Luke 10:42). Mary loved to learn and was determined to not allow menial tasks to distract her from gaining knowledge from the master.

Courageously pursue knowledge by regularly implementing these four basic Bible study steps.

1. Pray and ask God to give you wisdom and understanding as you learn from his Word.
2. Observe God's Word by asking who, what, when, where, why, and how of each passage of Scripture.
3. Interpret God's Word by identifying timeless life lessons contained in each passage.

4. Apply God's Word by making specific changes in your life based on biblical lessons.

## Interpret

Jesus wants us to value our time spent with him and make learning from him a priority in our lives.

## Apply

Do you strive to apply your knowledge of God's Word to your everyday life? What biblical life principle will you apply to your life today?

## Pray

*Father, you know my desires, and you know where I struggle. Help me consistently pursue knowledge from you and courageously apply it to my everyday life situations.*

# STRENGTHEN YOUR BELIEF

## (DAMARIS)

When they heard Paul speak about the resurrection of the
dead, some laughed in contempt, but others said, "We want to
hear more about this later." That ended Paul's discussion with
them, but some joined him and became believers. Among
them were Dionysius, a member of the council, a woman
named Damaris, and others with them.

ACTS 17:32–34

*Pray*

*Lord, please give me guidance as I approach your
Word and learn from your precepts.*

*Observe*

Our belief in God sets us on a path of
sanctification—the process in which we grow in our
ability to act, react, and respond more like Christ. A
process that lasts a lifetime and moves at a pace based
on our personal desire to grow closer to God.

There will always be skeptics who deny God exists
and question the reliability of his Word. Yet that in no
way negates the reality of his existence or the validity of
the Bible. Numerous men and women interacted with

Jesus during the time of his ministry on earth. However, some still chose not to believe.

Through the presence of God's Holy Spirit, the infallibility of his Word, and the countless evidences we observe throughout creation, God has given us everything we need to believe in the reality of his existence, his constant closeness, his unconditional love, and his faithfulness. "For ever since the world was created, people have seen the earth and sky. Through everything God made, they can clearly see his invisible qualities—his eternal power and divine nature. So they have no excuse for not knowing God" (Romans 1:20).

When others turned away and ridiculed the apostle Paul's words, Damaris immediately joined him and became a believer.

Courageously strengthen your belief by implementing the following daily practices.

1. Commune with God through a quiet time of prayer.
2. Learn more about God by reading and listening to his Word.
3. Discuss your faith with other believers and challenge one another to grow spiritually.

4. Experience God by applying his
   Word to your everyday life.

## Interpret

God expects us to believe, even when we cannot see. It's up to us to strengthen our faith so we can withstand days when our belief is challenged.

## Apply

Do you struggle with unbelief in certain areas of your walk with God? Research your particular struggle today in a concordance or an appendix of a study Bible. Make notes of passages of Scripture that relate to your challenge and meditate on these verses.

## Pray

*Father, thank you for sending the Holy Spirit to lead me into all truth. Thank you for your mercy, grace, love, and forgiveness. Lord, I do believe—please help my unbelief.*

## Day 33

# TAKE ON A CHALLENGE

### (EUNICE KENNEDY SHRIVER)

I can do all things through Him who strengthens me.

PHILIPPIANS 4:13 NASB

### Pray

*Lord, remove my distractions and help me focus on truth from your Word.*

### Observe

The word *yes* can be a power-packed word.

Saying yes to positive challenges can be both exhilarating and intimidating—all at the same time. Whether we are saying yes to a new career, new ministry opportunity, or relationship, there can be excitement in the air and fear of failure in the back of our minds.

When we are willing to embrace worthwhile endeavors, the opportunities for personal, spiritual, emotional, and professional growth are abundant. Especially when we acknowledge we're unable to truly succeed on our own without God's help.

Saying yes takes courage. When we rely on the Lord for help, he will give us the courage we need to overcome any fear and insecurity. We must ask ourselves: *What's the worst thing that could happen if I take on this challenge?* Some of the most brilliant and successful people of all time have experienced failure and rejection—and as they did, they learned valuable lessons that allowed them to grow and prepare to better handle their next needed challenge.

In the 1950s and '60s, Eunice Kennedy Shriver noticed how people with disabilities were often treated unjustly. Deeply moved by the struggles her mentally challenged sister faced, Eunice was determined to find ways to help her succeed. Routinely placed in institutions and excluded from society, the disabled population was, and often still is today, neglected and ignored. Eunice saw something in them that many others did not; she recognized their many talents. She believed sports provided the perfect opportunity to bring all types of people together, so she developed a program that became the Special Olympics in 1968.

Courageously embrace God-given challenges by applying the following principles.

1. Consider each challenge as an opportunity to learn and grow.
2. Face your fears and adopt the courage God will give you.

3. Maintain a positive attitude and give each challenge your very best effort.
4. Trust God completely with your outcome and accept that he knows best.

## Interpret

God will give us everything we need to take on, endure, and persevere through any challenge he desires us to embrace.

## Apply

Is God calling you to take on a particular challenge? Ask him to reveal to you the first step you need to take. Take that step today, knowing God is with you every step of the way.

## Pray

*Father, you call me to embrace challenges and remain steadfast in my pursuit of your will. Help me trust you with those challenges and embrace the courage you supply in order to say yes.*

# PRACTICE HOSPITALITY

## (THE WIDOW OF ZAREPHATH)

Then the LORD said to Elijah, "Go and live in the village of
Zarephath, near the city of Sidon. I have instructed a widow there
to feed you." So he went to Zarephath. As he arrived at the gates
of the village, he saw a widow gathering sticks, and he asked her,
"Would you please bring me a little water in a cup?" As she was
going to get it, he called to her, "Bring me a bite of bread, too."

1 KINGS 17:8–11

## Pray

*Lord, open my mind to the Spirit of Truth as I read
and study your Word.*

## Observe

Hospitality is a spiritual discipline and an
expression of Christ-like love. Some of us possess it as
a spiritual gift. But regardless of whether we believe
we have the gift of hospitality or not, God encourages
us all to practice it. Simply put, hospitality is caring for
people. The apostle Paul tells us to "Always be eager to
practice hospitality" (Romans 12:13). Peter encourages
us to "Cheerfully share your home with those who need
a meal or a place to stay" (1 Peter 4:9), and the writer of

Hebrews reminds us to not "forget to show hospitality to strangers, for some who have done this have entertained angels without realizing it" (Hebrews 13:2).

It's easy to live a self-centered life, one that spends more time focused on caring for self rather than caring for others. But love is way too great a gift not to share it with others!

God prepared the heart of the widow at Zarephath to provide refuge for the prophet Elijah. Left alone to raise her son during a time of severe drought, this godly widow extended hospitality to Elijah, even when she was down to her last meal. She immediately got up to get water when Elijah requested it. In honor of her loving hospitality, God miraculously provided an abundance of food and met their needs throughout Elijah's three months' stay.

Courageously practice hospitality by regularly developing the following habits.

1. Look for opportunities to provide a meal for someone in need.
2. Find creative ways to welcome visitors or new neighbors.
3. Make it a habit to compliment others, even those you don't know.
4. Volunteer at a local food pantry, homeless shelter, or ministry.

## Interpret

God promises to provide for our needs, and he calls on us to share what we have with others.

## Apply

Is God calling you to prepare a meal or provide a place to stay for someone in need? What can you do today to answer God's calling?

## Pray

*Father, bring to my mind the people you want me to reach out to and help me to know how you want me to show them hospitality.*

# Day 35

# SUPPORT THE GOSPEL

## (JOANNA)

Soon afterward Jesus began a tour of the nearby towns and villages, preaching and announcing the Good News about the Kingdom of God. He took his twelve disciples with him, along with some women who had been cured of evil spirits and diseases. Among them were Mary Magdalene, from whom he had cast out seven demons; Joanna, the wife of Chuza, Herod's business manager; Susanna; and many others who were contributing from their own resources to support Jesus and his disciples.

LUKE 8:1–3

## Pray

*Lord, through the power of your Holy Spirit reveal your truth to me.*

## Observe

Our primary biblical command is to go and make disciples of all nations, baptizing them and teaching them to obey all Christ's commands (Matthew 28:19–20).

One of the most important components of our Christian faith is our dedication to carry the gospel to the ends of the earth. As a disciple of Christ, we are called to give of our time, talents, and resources to support the gospel.

God never meant for us to walk this life journey alone, without guidance, support, and encouragement. He gives us everything we need for ourselves and for his kingdom work. Each of us has something to contribute. Have you ever considered how much you have to offer in helping take the gospel to the ends of the earth?

In Luke chapter 8, we meet faithful women who, having personally experienced Jesus' healing power, were eager to serve the Lord. They did this by supporting Jesus and his disciples out of their personal resources. One such woman was Joanna, the wife of Herod's business manager. Joanna was a devoted disciple who modeled the art of self-sacrifice in order to support the spread of the gospel.

Courageously support the Gospel by implementing one or more of the following practices.

1. Share your faith with friends, loved ones, and strangers and invite them to receive Christ.
2. Volunteer your time at a local Christian ministry or missions organization.
3. Contribute financially toward local and international Christian missions.

4. Vote for political candidates that most closely align with God and his Word.

## Interpret

Out of gratitude for all Christ has done for us, we are to support the spread of the gospel in every way we can with our available resources.

## Apply

In what ways are you currently supporting the gospel? What other ways can you use your available resources to participate in proclaiming the gospel both locally and abroad?

## Pray

*Father, everything I have belongs to you. Help me see clearly the ways you desire for me to support the gospel—whether by giving of my time, my talents, and/ or my financial resources.*

## Day 36

# TAKE A NECESSARY RISK

## (BILQUIS SHEIKH)

Dear friends, don't be surprised at the fiery trials you are
going through, as if something strange were happening to you.
Instead, be very glad—for these trials make you partners with
Christ in his suffering, so that you will have the wonderful joy
of seeing his glory when it is revealed to all the world.

1 Peter 4:12–13

*Pray*

*Lord, let your Word be a light unto my path.*

*Observe*

Maybe you have a big decision to make or desire
to invest in a new relationship. Perhaps you have
a dream of starting a ministry or long to be bold in
sharing your faith. No matter what challenge is before
you, you will need God-given courage to take the
necessary risk.

Bilquis Sheikh was a wealthy Muslim woman who
had a personal encounter with Jesus that compelled
her to put her life at risk in order to follow Christ. In
her book, *I Dared to Call Him Father,* she describes the

experience that led her to surrender her life to Christ and shares accounts of her faith journey, including narrow escapes from death. Bilquis' courage to follow God and her willingness to put her relationship with him above all else is a timeless source of inspiration and encouragement to us to take necessary risks in following Christ.

With each new decision, relationship, and choice we make, we must pre-determine in our hearts that we will focus on pleasing God. When we firmly believe our decisions, relationships, and choices honor him, we can courageously take risks and remember God will be with us, and we can trust him with our outcome. God promises to take care of us and bless us when we seek his will (Daniel 3:30; Matthew 6:33).

Courageously take risks for God by embracing the following principles.

1. Follow God's prompting regardless of the risk.
2. Remember God is with you no matter what the circumstance.
3. Believe God's presence will guide you and his power will equip you.
4. Trust God completely to do what's best for your future and his kingdom.

## Interpret

God warns us to expect fiery trials. He calls us to embrace our suffering as partners with Christ, remembering the joy that will come when his glory is revealed.

## Apply

Are you willing to take a necessary risk to follow God? Share the gospel with boldness today, knowing the Holy Spirit will empower you as you seek to do his will.

## Pray

*Father, thank you for your promise to care for me and bless me as I seek your will. Help me remember your promises and rely on your presence as I take necessary risks to pursue your calling on my life.*

# RECOGNIZE YOUR ENEMY

### (JAEL)

Most blessed among women is Jael, the wife of Heber the
Kenite. May she be blessed above all women who live in
tents. Sisera asked for water, and she gave him milk. In a
bowl fit for nobles, she brought him yogurt. Then with her left
hand she reached for a tent peg, and with her right hand for
the workman's hammer. She struck Sisera with the hammer,
crushing his head. With a shattering blow, she pierced his
temples. … "LORD, may all your enemies die like Sisera! But
may those who love you rise like the sun in all its power!"
Then there was peace in the land for forty years.

JUDGES 5:24–26, 31

### Pray

*Lord, prepare my heart and mind and give me a
teachable spirit.*

### Observe

As Christians, we desire to trust God and walk by
faith, but sometimes living a life of courage is difficult.
Our adversary, satan, wants nothing more than to keep
us physically, emotionally, and spiritually weak so we are
unable to courageously fulfill the plans God has for us.

In the days of Deborah, Sisera, a man of war who had terrorized Israel for years, was tormenting the Jews. Jael, the wife of Heber, a descendant of Moses' brother-in-law, recognized the enemy of her people and courageously defeated him, freeing Israel from their cruel opponent (Judges 4:11, 17–24).

While we are not physically in a religious war, we are in a spiritual battle. Therefore, our hearts and minds must be trained to recognize the tactics of our enemy, so we can overcome the distractions and detours he puts in our path.

Recognize the tactics of satan to courageously prepare a proper defense.

1. Satan is a liar; therefore we must identify his lies, seek guidance from the Holy Spirit, and acquire truth from God's Word.
2. Satan uses people to attack us; therefore we must embrace God's unconditional love and overcome our insecurities by deepening our relationship with Jesus.
3. Satan sends false teachers to deceive us; therefore we must know truth by reading and studying God's Word.
4. Satan is a tempter; therefore we must invite godly people to help hold us accountable where we are vulnerable.

## Interpret

God wants us to recognize and defeat our enemy so we can embrace God's peace and pursue God's will.

## Apply

Do you recognize the schemes of satan in your life? What step will you take today that will protect yourself against his current attack?

## Pray

*Father, please help me recognize the lies of the enemy and give me wisdom and discernment as I strive to prevail in spite of his interference and courageously pursue your plans for my life.*

# PRAISE GOD

## (ANNA)

Anna, a prophet, was also there in the Temple. She was the daughter of Phanuel from the tribe of Asher, and she was very old. Her husband died when they had been married only seven years. Then she lived as a widow to the age of eighty-four. She never left the Temple but stayed there day and night, worshiping God with fasting and prayer. She came along just as Simeon was talking with Mary and Joseph, and she began praising God. She talked about the child to everyone who had been waiting expectantly for God to rescue Jerusalem.

LUKE 2:36–38

### Pray

*Lord, help me embrace all you teach me as I meditate on your Word.*

### Observe

Praise is not something we do only when God answers our prayers. Praise arises out of our overwhelming love for our Savior, the one who created all things and goes with us and guides us through every life situation.

It's easy to praise God when things go our way,

but it's difficult to praise him when we're suffering, mistreated, abandoned, or abused. It's times like these when praise must be intentional—when we must lift up our voices in praise to him knowing all things will work together for good when we love him and pursue his purposes (Romans 8:28).

Praising God helps us see beyond our current circumstances, helps us embrace the joy that can only come from a personal relationship with Christ, and gives us the ability to face our challenges with courage and confidence.

Luke describes Anna as a widow who dedicated her life to service, praise, and worship. She was married for only seven years and remained a widow the rest of her life. When tragedy struck, Anna chose to praise God in spite of her circumstances.

Courageously praise God in the following ways.

1. Meditate on the attributes of God and praise him for his majesty (1 Chronicles 29:11).
2. Acknowledge God's sovereign control and praise him for his promises (Jeremiah 29:11).
3. Thank God for the light he provides in the midst of the darkness (John 1:4–5).
4. Celebrate God's unconditional, undeserved, extravagant love (Romans 8:38–39).

### Interpret

We are to serve, worship, pray, and praise even when our circumstances aren't what we hoped for.

### Apply

Are you in the middle of a life crisis? Are you finding it hard to praise God? Go to God in prayer today—praise him for his presence, acknowledge your struggle, and ask him to give you guidance and hope.

### Pray

*Father, I praise you for your unconditional love, mercy, and grace. Please heal my heart when it's broken, lift up my spirit when it is wounded, and give me hope when I am hopeless.*

# TRY SOMETHING NEW

## (MARY KAY ASH)

Don't copy the behavior and customs of this world, but let God transform you into a new person by changing the way you think. Then you will learn to know God's will for you, which is good and pleasing and perfect.

ROMANS 12:2

*Pray*

*Lord, open my eyes to your truth and help me understand and obey your precepts.*

*Observe*

Most of us don't like change. We get comfortable with the familiar and accept the status quo, even when it's not in our best interest. We like our routines and dislike uncertainty. But God doesn't call us to barricade ourselves into a comfort zone. He wants us to try new things and embrace new opportunities.

As we engage in new endeavors, we establish new relationships and are given new opportunities to minister to others. When we make it a habit to regularly try something new, we become more willing to change and more open to God's desired direction for our lives.

Mary Kay Ash believed in the Golden Rule: "Do to others whatever you would like them to do to you" (Matthew 7:12). She operated by the motto: God first, family second, and career third. After being passed over for a promotion that was given to a man she had trained, Mary Kay decided to write a book for women in business. Her book turned into a business plan that ultimately ranked one of the top one hundred best companies to work for in America, and one of the top ten best companies for women—Mary Kay, Inc. Her vision, courage, and willingness to try something new continue to help women achieve their potential and bring their dreams to life to this very day.

Courageously try something new by accepting the following truths.

1. God expects you to be careful how you live and make the most of every opportunity he sends your way (Ephesians 5:15–17).
2. God expects you to trust him, seek his will, and follow his lead (Proverbs 3:5–6).
3. God will equip you to do his will through the power of Jesus Christ (Hebrews 13:21).
4. God expects you to turn away from sin, remove any obstacle standing in your way, and pursue with endurance the direction he is calling you to go (Hebrews 12:1).

### Interpret

At times, God directs his people toward a new and unfamiliar path. His desire is that we embrace this new direction and trust him to prepare the way.

### Apply

Name one thing new you sense God calling you to try and step out in faith and start trying it today.

### Pray

*Father, thank you for preparing a new way for me. Please give me the courage and confidence to embrace the opportunities you send my way.*

# BE PATIENT

## (SARAH)

The LORD kept his word and did for Sarah exactly what he had promised. She became pregnant, and she gave birth to a son for Abraham in his old age. This happened at just the time God had said it would. And Abraham named their son Isaac. Eight days after Isaac was born, Abraham circumcised him as God had commanded. Abraham was 100 years old when Isaac was born. And Sarah declared, "God has brought me laughter. All who hear about this will laugh with me. Who would have said to Abraham that Sarah would nurse a baby? Yet I have given Abraham a son in his old age!"

GENESIS 21:1–7

## Pray

*Lord, give me a heart of understanding and a genuine desire for a deeper knowledge of you.*

## Observe

Throughout God's Word, we see examples of his patience with mankind and his call on humanity to practice patience. Because God is patient with us, so must we be patient—patient with ourselves, patient with others, patient with our plans, and patient with our lives in general. When you're tempted to be impatient with something or someone, think about how patient God has been with you and how he is leading you through life his way—in his timing.

Sarah and Abraham were married many years, but their one great heartache was that they had no children. Abraham and Sarah accepted God's Word when he promised to make them the father and mother of many nations, but they were both very old and had no heir. Patience was a requirement for Sarah, and although she regrettably interfered with God's plan for a time, God honored her faithful waiting by giving her a son at the age of ninety.

Be courageously patient by memorizing the following passages.

1. "Those who trust in the LORD will find new strength" (Isaiah 40:31).
2. "Be still in the presence of the LORD, and wait patiently for him to act" (Psalm 37:7).
3. "Finishing is better than starting. Patience is better than pride" (Ecclesiastes 7:8).
4. "Warn those who are lazy. Encourage those who are timid. Take tender care of those who are weak. Be patient with everyone" (1 Thessalonians 5:14).

## Interpret

God's plans are perfect plans, but they require his people to wait patiently on his perfect timing.

## Apply

Are you struggling to be patient while waiting for God to answer your prayer or grant a request? Make a commitment today to trust God's will and wait for him, knowing his timing is perfect and worth the wait.

## Pray

*Father, give me strength to fully surrender my hopes, dreams, and prayers over to your sovereign control and help me to accept your will and trust in your timing.*

# HELP THE HELPLESS

## (PHARAOH'S DAUGHTER)

Soon Pharaoh's daughter came down to bathe in the river, and her attendants walked along the riverbank. When the princess saw the basket among the reeds, she sent her maid to get it for her. When the princess opened it, she saw the baby. The little boy was crying, and she felt sorry for him. "This must be one of the Hebrew children," she said. Then the baby's sister approached the princess. "Should I go and find one of the Hebrew women to nurse the baby for you?" she asked. "Yes, do!" the princess replied. So the girl went and called the baby's mother. "Take this baby and nurse him for me," the princess told the baby's mother. "I will pay you for your help." So the woman took her baby home and nursed him.

EXODUS 2:5–9

*Pray*

*Lord, open the eyes of my heart and help me discern truth from your Word.*

*Observe*

God created us to care for one another. We are made in his image—masterfully designed to care for and love others in the same way God cares for and loves us.

Throughout the Bible, we are commanded to look out for the interests of others, be kind, tenderhearted and loving, to not grow weary in doing good, but to be generous and compassionate, and to build one another up (Philippians 2:4; Ephesians 4:32; Galatians 6:9; Proverbs 19:17; Colossians 3:12; 1 Thessalonians 5:11). God makes it clear, as we care for and serve others, we are actually caring for and serving him (Matthew 25:35; Ephesians 6:7).

In Exodus chapter 2, we are introduced to a kind, tenderhearted, and compassionate daughter of a cruel ruler. Pharaoh's daughter likely risked repercussions from her father who had commanded the drowning of all male Hebrew babies. Through her compassionate desire to help the helpless, she saved the child who was chosen by God to become one of Israel's greatest heroes.

Courageously help the helpless by embracing the following opportunities on a regular basis:

1. Personally minister to someone who is sick, hungry, rejected, or hurting.
2. Support a local foster care program.
3. Contribute to a food pantry.
4. Donate clothes to a local clothing ministry.

## Interpret

God deeply loves mankind and commands us to love and care for one another in the same way that he loves and cares for us.

## Apply

Is there someone in need who God has placed on your heart? Reach out to them today and make an effort to help meet their need.

## Pray

*Father, give me compassion for those around me who are in need. Help me to know how I am to meet their needs and direct my steps as I strive to make a difference.*

# CHOOSE GOD'S VIEW

## (GIANNA JESSEN)

You made all the delicate, inner parts of my body and knit me together in my mother's womb. Thank you for making me so wonderfully complex! Your workmanship is marvelous—how well I know it. You watched me as I was being formed in utter seclusion, as I was woven together in the dark of the womb. You saw me before I was born. Every day of my life was recorded in your book. Every moment was laid out before a single day had passed.

PSALM 139:13–16

*Pray*

*Lord, give me the ability to see the wondrous truth in your Word.*

*Observe*

God knows who we are, where we are, and what we're doing at all times; he loves us unconditionally right in the midst of it all. As believers, we must embrace the facts that our past doesn't define us, our success or failure can't define us, the opinions of others won't define us, and what we have or don't have will never define us.

It is God—and only God—who defines us.

Gianna Jessen, scheduled to be one of the multitudes of abortions that take place in the United States each year, miraculously survived her intended fate, spent several months in the hospital, and eventually ended up in foster care. The failed abortion left Gianna with cerebral palsy. Doctors declared her a hopeless case, and they predicted she would likely never raise her head. But God's view of Gianna was very different from the world's view, and today she not only lifts her head to praise Jesus, but she also runs marathons, shares the gospel, and uses her unshakable faith and testimony to inspire people all around the world. Gianna passionately proclaims, "My goal is to live the impossible since nothing is impossible for God."

Courageously choose God's view of you by embracing the following truths.

1. I am made in the image of God (Genesis 1:26–27).
2. I am fearfully and wonderfully made (Psalm 139:14).
3. I am a new person in Christ and my new life has begun (2 Corinthians 5:17).
4. I am chosen by God and my identity is in him (1 Peter 2:9).

## Interpret

God delicately and attentively created each person. He has ordained each day of our lives and is with us each moment of our day.

## Apply

Take note of how God sees you and how you view yourself. Decide today to set aside any negative thoughts you have about yourself and live in light of God's loving view of you.

## Pray

*Father, thank you for giving me new life and purpose. Grant me the ability to lay aside negative thoughts and help me fully embrace my God-given value and uniqueness.*

*Day 43*

# RECEIVE GRACE

## (BATHSHEBA)

Then on the seventh day the child died. … Then David
comforted Bathsheba, his wife, and slept with her. She became
pregnant and gave birth to a son, and David named him
Solomon. The LORD loved the child and sent word through
Nathan the prophet that they should name him Jedidiah
(which means "beloved of the LORD"), as the LORD had
commanded.

2 SAMUEL 12:18, 24–25

*Pray*

*Lord, fill me with awe and wonder as I study your
Word and meditate on your precepts.*

*Observe*

Grace is an extravagant gift from God—a gift many of
us find extremely difficult to understand, let alone accept.

Grace is not a one-time, name it and claim it
event. Once we're saved, we are a new creation; old
things have passed away, and new things have come (2
Corinthians 5:17). Therefore, let's keep God's grace from
being in vain by learning to embrace it fully, do away
with our self-condemnation, and be reconciled to God.

Let's turn away from our sin and pursue a life worthy of his amazing grace.

The best way to fully receive God's grace is to set aside our need to hold on to our mistakes or painful memories. We need to unpack our negative baggage and willingly accept God's grace and love without self-condemnation, fear, and shame.

Bathsheba suffered severe consequences as a result of David's sin. But she embraced God's grace and steadfast love, and her life was restored. Bathsheba and David went on to have many children, one of whom was Solomon, King of Israel, who became a forefather of Christ (Matthew 1).

Courageously receive God's grace by accepting the following truths.

1. The Lord is close to the broken hearted; he rescues those whose spirits are crushed (Psalm 34:18).
2. Christ has truly set you free (Galatians 5:1).
3. God chose you before the foundation of the earth to be holy and blameless (Ephesians 1:4).
4. Because you have confessed your sin, God has forgiven you and cleansed you from all unrighteousness (1 John 1:9).

God freely and abundantly offers grace—it's just up to us to receive it, embrace it, and encourage others to embrace it as well.

## Interpret

God's amazing grace grants us forgiveness for our sins and restoration in our lives.

## Apply

Have you received God's gracious forgiveness, and are you living a restored life? Accept your restoration today and walk courageously in your newfound freedom.

## Pray

*Father, help me embrace your grace and walk in light of my relationship with you. Give me the courage to receive grace and the ability to extend it to others.*

# PREPARE FOR TEMPTATION

## (EVE)

The serpent was the shrewdest of all the wild animals the LORD
God had made. One day he asked the woman, "Did God
really say you must not eat the fruit from any of the trees in
the garden?" "Of course we may eat fruit from the trees in the
garden," the woman replied. "It's only the fruit from the tree
in the middle of the garden that we are not allowed to eat.
God said, 'You must not eat it or even touch it; if you do, you
will die.'" "You won't die!" the serpent replied to the woman.
"God knows that your eyes will be opened as soon as you eat
it, and you will be like God, knowing both good and evil."

GENESIS 3:1–5

*Pray*

*Lord, give me a hunger for your Word and a desire
to walk worthy of your calling.*

*Observe*

God's Word speaks of temptation often and warns
us to watch and pray so we might not fall (Matthew
26:41; Mark 14:38; Luke 22:40; Luke 22:46). We
don't have to look hard to see the world's enticements:
material possessions, relationships, prestige, power,

control, and food. Temptation comes in all types, shapes, and sizes.

Our spirit tells us to flee, but our flesh is weak and wants us to give in. God never promises we won't be tempted, but he does promise to provide a way of escape (1 Corinthians 10:13).

God placed Adam and Eve in the garden, giving them everything they needed for a perfect life. But satan, in his clever deception, convinced Eve to disobey God. Using the same tactics he uses today, he questioned her understanding of God's Word and seduced her with the beauty of the fruit and the promise of wisdom.

Courageously overcome temptation by implementing the following steps.

1. Be filled and led by the Holy Spirit just as Jesus was when he resisted satan's temptations (Luke 4:1–2).
2. Know God's Word just as Jesus did when he countered satan's lies with the truth (Luke 4:3–4).
3. Obey God and serve him only just as Jesus did (Luke 4:5–12).
4. Be alert and aware always that satan is on the prowl for an opportune time to tempt us (Luke 4:13).

## Interpret

Satan is rarely obvious in his pursuit to deceive us. If we don't recognize his subtle lies, we are vulnerable to be drawn into sin.

## Apply

What area of your life is most vulnerable to sin? What step will you take today to strengthen your resistance to temptation?

## Pray

*Father, give me wisdom and insight to recognize my areas of vulnerability and help me sufficiently prepare so I can courageously turn away from temptation to sin.*

# CONSIDER YOUR CONVERSATIONS

## (SUSANNA WESLEY)

Don't use foul or abusive language. Let everything you say be good and helpful, so that your words will be an encouragement to those who hear them.

EPHESIANS 4:29

*Pray*

*Lord, help me to hunger and thirst for your promises found in your Word.*

*Observe*

There is power in the spoken word. Power to build up, encourage, and honor, and power to tear down, discourage, and slander. Our words expose our attitudes and have the ability to represent our character. A word can alter the outcome of a court case. Have you ever stopped to think how even the smallest of words can change your conversations? Unfortunately, we often find ourselves using unnecessary words that turn our conversations in negative directions.

For example, we might take responsibility for our role in the dispute by stating, "I was wrong, and I let you down," then attempt to justify our poor behavior by inserting the word *but*—"but I had a lot going on at the time." Many times we are more concerned with defending our behavior and less worried about how our actions and words negatively impact those around us.

Children are greatly influenced by our words. Friends and loved ones can be deeply moved or emotionally hurt by our words, and co-workers or employees can be motivated or discouraged by our words. The wrong words can cause conversations to quickly turn negative. Therefore, we must choose our words carefully and navigate our communication sensibly.

Susanna Wesley considered her nineteen children the greatest gifts from God. In spite of marital difficulties, the death of several children, and devastating poverty, she maintained her character and deepened her faith in Christ. Though she authored no books nor traveled the world publicly speaking, the biblical lessons she wrote and the words she spoke greatly motivated her children, two of whom later influenced millions throughout the world as a result of their preaching and teaching. She was the mother of John and Charles Wesley, two of the greatest evangelists to ever walk the earth.

Courageously watch your words by remembering these important truths.

1. By your words you will be justified or condemned (Matthew 12:37).
2. Your words have consequences, leading to life or death (Proverbs 18:19).
3. Your words have the power to accomplish good purposes (Isaiah 55:11).
4. You will give an account for every careless word you speak (Matthew 12:36).

## Interpret

God expects us to watch what we say and be a positive, godly influence to those who hear us.

## Apply

Carefully watch your words and see how many people you can encourage today.

## Pray

*Father, thank you for reminding me that my words influence those around me. Help me speak words of encouragement and inspiration.*

*Day 46*

# ASK QUESTIONS

(WOMAN AT THE WELL)

"But sir, you don't have a rope or a bucket," she said, "and this well is very deep. Where would you get this living water?" … Jesus replied, "Anyone who drinks this water will soon become thirsty again. But those who drink the water I give will never be thirsty again. It becomes a fresh, bubbling spring within them, giving them eternal life." "Please, sir," the woman said, "give me this water! Then I'll never be thirsty again, and I won't have to come here to get water."

JOHN 4:11, 13–15

*Pray*

*Lord, open my eyes to your truth and help me understand and obey your precepts.*

*Observe*

Knowing what right questions to ask is often more important than having all the answers. Have you ever experienced conversations that get off track or interviews that are less than productive? Could it be that you're asking the wrong questions—or you're not asking questions at all?

By asking thoughtful questions, we encourage

others to open up. They are more likely to share personal information, talk about what they believe, and discuss why they believe the way they do. Our questions can inspire others to think about their thinking and consider their worldview.

Asking the right questions also helps us learn more about people, places, and things that impact our everyday lives. When we are more informed about our surroundings, we are better prepared to make wise choices and decisions.

The Samaritan woman was surprised when Jesus began to talk with her. She immediately began by asking him questions and listened attentively to his answers. By asking and listening, the Samaritan woman learned Christ's identity and discovered the source of eternal life. As a result, she received salvation and was prepared to share the gospel with her entire village.

Throughout his ministry, Jesus frequently asked questions when teaching and answered questions in his lessons.

Courageously ask questions by practicing the following steps.

1. **Plan**. Reflect on the topic of a conversation; consider all points and possibilities.
2. **Prepare**. Consider questions you can ask to gain understanding and new information.

3. **Pray**. Ask God for wisdom and
   discernment during the conversation.
4. **Be Patient**. Listen carefully and
   wait for the opportune time to ask your
   questions.

*Interpret*

Jesus wants us to ask questions, listen attentively,
and respond appropriately.

*Apply*

Are you willing to stop talking and ask powerful
questions? Prepare several questions for a conversation
you will have with a friend, loved one, or godly advisor
today.

*Pray*

*Father, you know the plans you have for my
future. Help me to ask the right questions so I can gain
understanding, learn new information, and make better
decisions.*

# TRUST GOD

## (JOCHEBED, MOTHER OF MOSES)

Then Pharaoh gave this order to all his people: "Throw every newborn Hebrew boy into the Nile River. But you may let the girls live." About this time, a man and woman from the tribe of Levi got married. The woman became pregnant and gave birth to a son. She saw that he was a special baby and kept him hidden for three months. But when she could no longer hide him, she got a basket made of papyrus reeds and waterproofed it with tar and pitch. She put the baby in the basket and laid it among the reeds along the bank of the Nile River.

Exodus 1:22–2:3

## *Pray*

*Lord, enlighten my mind with truth as I seek inspiration and guidance from your Word.*

## *Observe*

When you get anxious, do you go into control mode—thinking of all the ways you can fix your problems? Sometimes we even try to fix everyone else's problems as well. In stressful times like these, the Lord will often remind us to relax because he has everything under control.

We can trust God with our lives and the lives of those we love. We can be confident he knows best, can handle our problems, and will work all things together for good (Romans 8:38). There's no need to worry. After all, worrying never improves our situation; it wastes our time, and it can wreak havoc on our health.

God will never lead us astray and will always lead us the best way!

Trusting God ushers in hope (Jeremiah 29:11), brings comfort (2 Corinthians 1:4), provides clarity (Proverbs 3:6), grants confidence (Proverbs 14:26), gives reassurance (Romans 10:11), supplies security (Psalm 91), and produces peace (Philippians 4:6–7). Therefore, we must trust God instead of ourselves. We must trust God rather than other people. And trust God in spite of our circumstances.

Jochebed, mother to three gifted leaders during Israel's Exodus, trusted God's providence, protection, and love. Desperate to fight for the life of her baby boy, Moses, she put him in a wicker basket and courageously hid him along the bank of the Nile River. Jochebed trusted God and his plan for her son's life.

## Interpret

We can trust God with our lives and the lives of those we love.

## Apply

Is there something or someone you need to let go of and give to God? Make a commitment today to trust God completely and embrace the peace and reassurance that comes from knowing he is in control.

## Pray

*Father, I am eternally grateful for your love and faithfulness. Please help me to surrender my need for control and give me the courage to fully trust you with the situations and circumstances that worry me.*

# BEGIN WITH PRAYER

## (FANNY CROSBY)

Pray like this: Our Father in heaven, may your name be kept holy. May your Kingdom come soon. May your will be done on earth, as it is in heaven. Give us today the food we need, and forgive us our sins, as we have forgiven those who sin against us. And don't let us yield to temptation, but rescue us from the evil one.

MATTHEW 6:9–13

## Pray

*Lord, give me a heart of understanding and a genuine desire for a deeper knowledge of you.*

## Observe

Much too often, we neglect to pray until tragedy strikes, or we need God's forgiveness, or we're seeking his help. Yet we miss out on so much if we seldom pray. Our prayers allow us to communicate intimately with our heavenly father. They invite God into our day and welcome him into our endeavors. Throughout God's Word, we are called to pray. Prayer has power over evil, and it allows us to experience greater intimacy with God. More than one hundred times, God's Word speaks of prayer.

Prayer is not a guarantee that suffering won't come, but an opportunity to embrace God's presence in the midst of all circumstances. It allows us to seek and discern God's will and prepares our hearts for obedience and adoration. The Christian life is full of blessings and rewards, but one of the greatest gifts of all is our direct access to our Lord and Savior through prayer.

Frances Jane van Alstyne, better known as Fanny Crosby, was an American missionary, poet, hymnist, and composer. Fanny began each daily endeavor in prayer with the Lord, confident that she needed God's help to inspire her creativity and achieve her goals. Despite being totally blind from early childhood, Fanny became a very gifted and prolific hymnist, writing over 9,000 hymns, many still sung in our churches to this very day.

Courageously begin each day and endeavor in prayer realizing the following important truths.

1. Your prayers will help you resist temptation (Matthew 26:41).
2. You will receive mercy and grace each time you pray (Hebrews 4:13).
3. Your prayers acknowledge your faith in God's sovereignty (Philippians 4:6–7).
4. Your prayers have the power to heal and produce wondrous results (James 5:16).

## Interpret

Jesus calls us to pray with thanksgiving and praise, acknowledging God for his majesty, forgiveness, provisions, and kingdom.

## Apply

Take time today to thank God for your many blessings and the forgiveness of your sins. Acknowledge his power and provisions and request his wisdom and guidance.

## Pray

*Father, thank you for allowing me to come boldly before your throne in prayer. Help me recognize my need for greater intimacy with you and compel me to rely faithfully on your guiding hand.*

# LISTEN ATTENTIVELY

## (PRISCILLA)

Meanwhile, a Jew named Apollos, an eloquent speaker who knew the Scriptures well, had arrived in Ephesus from Alexandria in Egypt. He had been taught the way of the Lord, and he taught others about Jesus with an enthusiastic spirit and with accuracy. However, he knew only about John's baptism. When Priscilla and Aquila heard him preaching boldly in the synagogue, they took him aside and explained the way of God even more accurately.

ACTS 18:24–26

### Pray

*Lord, open the eyes of my heart and help me discern truth from your Word.*

### Observe

Genuine communication happens when we listen thoughtfully and respond appropriately.

There is a big difference between hearing and listening. Hearing is the process of perceiving sound, and listening is paying careful attention in order to hear what is being said, sung, or played.

If we desire to influence, guide, or instruct others,

it is vitally important we *listen* rather than simply hear what they are saying. Too often, we are so consumed with our need to talk we barely let others get their words out before jumping in with our insights and opinions. Other times, we are so busy thinking about how to respond that we neglect to pay attention to what is actually being said. Attentive listening is vital in establishing a healthy environment for communication.

Priscilla and her husband, Aquila, invited the apostle Paul to live with them during his eighteen-month stay in Corinth. No doubt they listened attentively to Paul's teaching and grew deep in their knowledge of Christ. They were well prepared to help open the eyes of Apollos as they carefully listened to him speak and realized he only knew of Christ's baptism by John. When they lovingly shared truth with Apollos, he listened intently and soon became a great gospel preacher.

Courageously listen attentively by implementing the following attributes into your next conversation.

1. Allow others to complete their thoughts without interruption.
2. Focus on what others are saying and avoid distractions.
3. Strive to understand the other person's point-of-view before sharing yours.

4. Communicate genuine care while listening and speak truth in love when responding.

## Interpret

When we listen attentively to others and carefully discern their comprehension of God's truth, we can then inspire them to grow stronger in their knowledge and understanding of God and his Word.

## Apply

Practice listening attentively in your next conversation today. Ask questions and carefully consider their responses. Then share your insights by communicating with care.

## Pray

*Father, help me patiently listen as others share their beliefs. Give me the courage to speak boldly about my faith and the desire to inspire others in their knowledge of you and your Word.*

# RENEW YOUR MIND

## (QUEEN OF SHEBA)

When the queen of Sheba heard of Solomon's fame, which brought honor to the name of the LORD, she came to test him with hard questions. ... She exclaimed to the king, "Everything I heard in my country about your achievements and wisdom is true! I didn't believe what was said until I arrived here and saw it with my own eyes. In fact, I had not heard the half of it! Your wisdom and prosperity are far beyond what I was told." ... "Praise the LORD your God, who delights in you and has placed you on the throne of Israel. Because of the LORD's eternal love for Israel, he has made you king so you can rule with justice and righteousness."

1 KINGS 10:1, 6–7, 9

## Pray

*Lord, let me clearly observe truth in your Word and properly apply it to my life.*

## Observe

We all have beliefs. Beliefs about what we think matters, why we exist, and what direction we need to go. Beliefs about who God is and who we are. Beliefs we adopt throughout life from parents, teachers, loved ones, and friends.

The important thing to understand about beliefs is they significantly impact the everyday choices we make. Therefore, it's important we make sure our convictions are grounded in truth and measured by God's Word.

The queen of Sheba came to Jerusalem to see for herself the profound wisdom of Solomon. Her eagerness to know truth inspired her conversation and her desire to talk with Solomon about everything she had on her mind (10:2). She was moved by the truth, allowed it to penetrate her heart, and, as a result, will stand among believers on the day of judgment (Matthew 12:42).

Courageously renew your mind by answering the following questions and reading the corresponding truth.

1. Is it better for me to hide my pain and problems from other people? (James 5:16)
2. Do I need to care for others and neglect my own God-given needs? (Matthew 22:39)
3. Am I responsible for the actions and behaviors of others? (Ezekiel 18:20)
4. Do I need the approval of others to be valuable? (Galatians 1:10)

## Interpret

God, the giver of wisdom, empowers believers by his Word. Others are drawn to truth and are inspired by God's love for his people.

## Apply

Open your Bible today, read one or more of the passages listed above, and ask God to reveal truth to you through his Word.

## Pray

*Father, you tell me in your Word not to believe everything I hear, and you warn me to test all things before adopting them as truth. Please guide me to the truth and remind me to use the Bible as a plumb line.*

## Day 51

# BE RESTORED

### (ALVEDA C. KING)

Now repent of your sins and turn to God, so that your sins
may be wiped away. Then times of refreshment will come from
the presence of the Lord, and he will again send you Jesus,
your appointed Messiah.

ACTS 3:19–20

### Pray

*Lord, let your Word be a mirror into my soul.*

### Observe

God encourages us to grieve, mourn, and allow
ourselves to feel our pain—then turn to him so he
can heal our pain and restore our souls. Many of the
Psalmists describe periods of deep grief and cried out to
God for relief and deliverance.

Grief comes in all shapes and sizes. Whether
we are grieving over our own sin or sin that has been
committed against us, our grief is processed through
various stages and is experienced in unique ways based
on our individual personalities. Grief can take our
breath away and leave us feeling deeply guilty, sad,
fearful, and regretful.

God doesn't want us to stay in a place of pain forever. He calls us to take refuge within his loving arms. His grace is sufficient (2 Corinthians 12:9), his comfort is real (2 Corinthians 1:3-4), he can use all things for good (Romans 8:28), and there is hope for our future (Hebrews 10:23). By willfully embracing God's mercy and grace, our joy can be restored and our outlook can be hopeful.

Alveda C. King shared her testimony of God's loving restoration after having two abortions. Niece of the late civil rights activist Dr. Martin Luther King Jr., Alveda became a pro-life champion after Jesus transformed her life. Today she helps many women heal by sharing her testimony and currently serves as director and pastoral associate of Civil Rights for the Unborn as well as director of African American Outreach for Gospel of Life. Nothing stops this courageous woman from speaking up for the value of life, and she urges others to boldly do the same.

Courageously be restored by exercising the following principles.

1. Pour your heart out to God and let him be your refuge (Psalm 62:8).
2. Allow God to renew your strength (Psalm 23:1–6).

3. Reach out to others for godly support and encouragement (1 Thessalonians 5:11).
4. Trust God to heal your broken heart and restore your broken life (Psalm 147:3).

## Interpret

God calls his followers to turn away from sin and turn to him so their sins will be forgiven and their souls will be restored.

## Apply

Confess your sin and receive God's healing today and let the experience shine through in your attitude toward yourself and your temperament around others.

## Pray

*Father, thank you for the forgiveness of my sins and restoration of my soul. Help me fully embrace your grace and give me the ability to live in light of your mercy.*

# EMBRACE ACCEPTANCE

## (RUTH)

When Naomi saw that Ruth was determined to go with her, she said nothing more. So the two of them continued on their journey. When they came to Bethlehem, the entire town was excited by their arrival. "Is it really Naomi?" the women asked. "Don't call me Naomi," she responded. "Instead, call me Mara, for the Almighty has made life very bitter for me."

RUTH 1:18–20

## Pray

*Lord, teach me from your Word and help me to walk in your ways.*

## Observe

God's Word teaches us to be content in our circumstances, to identify and overcome issues that negatively impact our lives, and to discern the difference between what God wants us to accept and what he wants us to change.

When it comes to accepting our situations or circumstances, we need to evaluate each event separately. When it comes to accepting people in our life, there's an essential factor we must consider. While we can encourage and influence the beliefs, behaviors, actions, and reactions of others, we cannot change them.

Embracing acceptance doesn't mean we simply settle for the way things are. It means we consider each situation or relationship prayerfully, seek solutions that honor God, and courageously choose a Christ-like response.

We learn a lot about the art of acceptance from the life of Ruth. She couldn't change the fact her husband, father-in-law, and brother-in-law were deceased. And she couldn't change the fact her mother-in-law had no other option than to leave Moab, the only home Ruth had ever known. But Ruth could courageously choose to accept her reality, seek a God-honoring solution, and make a godly choice—which she did.

Courageously embrace acceptance by practicing the following.

1. Memorize the following portion of the Serenity Prayer by Reinhold Niebuhr: "God, grant me the serenity to accept the things I cannot change, courage to change the things I can, and wisdom to know the difference."
2. Pray for the wisdom to discern the things you can and cannot change.
3. Journal your appraisal of the things you can and cannot change.

4. Ask God to give you the courage to
   accept your reality, the wisdom to discover
   God-honoring solutions, and the ability to
   make godly decisions.

## Interpret

We are to accept the circumstances we cannot
change, seek God-honoring solutions in all situations,
and strive to make decisions that honor God.

## Apply

Is there a situation or circumstance you cannot
change? Ask God today to help you accept your reality
and give you wisdom in making decisions.

## Pray

*Father, give me the courage to accept the
situations, circumstances, and people in my life I need
to accept and give me the wisdom to find solutions and
make decisions that honor you.*

## Day 53

# TAKE UP FOR TRUTH

## (EUODIA AND SYNTYCHE)

Now I appeal to Euodia and Syntyche. Please, because you
belong to the Lord, settle your disagreement. And I ask you,
my true partner, to help these two women, for they worked
hard with me in telling others the Good News. They worked
along with Clement and the rest of my co-workers, whose
names are written in the Book of Life.

PHILIPPIANS 4:2–3

### Pray

*Lord, remove my distractions and help me focus on
truth from your Word.*

### Observe

We are blessed to live in a country where our rights
and freedoms are protected. Yet we are often pressured
to choose political correctness over biblical truth. To
protect the feelings of others with opposing views, we are
commonly tempted to keep quiet about our faith when
we find ourselves in a crowd among non-believers.

God wants to be first in our lives. He wants to be
our primary focus. He desires to strengthen our faith
and grow our courage muscles so we can stand firm in

our convictions and take up for his truth. Too often, we allow our culture to impact us—rather than impacting our culture for the sake of the gospel.

Even though we are *in the world*, we are called to reject its enticement to become *of the world*. We are to be set apart, noticeably different from non-believers (Colossians 3:10), and ready to be used by God for every good work (2 Timothy 2:21).

The apostle Paul urged Euodia and Syntyche to give up their differences and focus on their evangelistic calling. Paul praised them for sharing the good news of Christ in a Roman colony where a large number of gods were worshiped. Euodia and Syntyche passionately embraced the gospel and boldly took up for truth by consistently sharing their faith with others.

Courageously stand up for your faith by implementing the following steps.

1. Pray and ask God to prepare you to share your faith with others.
2. Memorize 1 Corinthians 16:13 and faithfully embrace your God-given courage.
3. Look for opportunities to share your faith; ask someone about their beliefs, offer to pray for someone's needs, or invite someone to church.

4. Take action and share your faith in
   a loving way—even if you're afraid.

## Interpret

God is honored and the body of Christ celebrates when we work in harmony to defend the gospel and share God's truth.

## Apply

Practice speaking up for truth today by initiating a conversation about Christ with a stranger.

## Pray

*Father, it is by your power I can overcome opposition when my beliefs are challenged. Give me the ability to stand firm in my faith and the courage to boldly speak truth to lost people I encounter.*

# APPRECIATE CREATION

## (JENNIFER WISEMAN)

For ever since the world was created, people have seen the earth and sky. Through everything God made, they can clearly see his invisible qualities—his eternal power and divine nature. So they have no excuse for not knowing God.

ROMANS 1:20

## Pray

Lord, give me wisdom and understanding of you and your precepts as I study your Word.

## Observe

God's very first words to us in the Bible are the account of creation. Yet how often do we really consider the magnificence of his handiwork? How the sun gives light and warmth to our earth, and the moon controls the ocean's tides. How the stars shine like diamonds in the sky, and clouds bring shade and badly needed rain. God is by far the greatest artist, scientist, and mathematician of all time—yet we often overlook these astounding attributes.

God's true masterpiece is clearly seen in the

intricacies of you and me. When we look at ourselves—and others, we need to appreciate the life God created and see the possibilities within his work-in-progress, rather than focusing on the faults and flaws that tend to cloud our view.

Jennifer Wiseman grew up on a farm in Arkansas appreciating the night sky and God's creativity in creation. She clearly recognizes the cohesion between God and nature and is passionate about sharing her love of creation and science with others. Today Jennifer is an astrophysicist and senior project scientist for NASA, where her primary responsibility is making sure the Hubble Space Telescope is successful in its mission. Jennifer is also program director of Dialogue on Science, Ethics, and Religion for the American Association for the Advancement of Science, an organization that encourages communication between scientists and religious communities throughout the world.

Courageously appreciate God's creation by adopting the following practices.

1. Take time each day to walk outside and take in the beauty of God's creation.
2. Consciously consider the complexities of everything God has created.
3. Make a commitment to care for one of the pinnacles of God's creation—you.

4. Show your appreciation for others God has created by ministering to their needs.

## Interpret

God's character and attributes are clearly seen through his creation. Therefore, no one has a legitimate excuse to doubt his existence.

## Apply

How often do you stop and consider the beauty and intricacy of God's creation? Spend time outside today—take a walk, visit a park, or take a scenic drive—and appreciate the beauty God allows us to experience.

## Pray

*Father, thank you for everything you created—for the oceans and the sky, the mountains and the valleys. Help me to regularly recognize and enjoy the beauty of heaven, earth, and all the people around me.*

# Day 55

# STOP WORRYING

## (MARY MAGDALENE)

The women were terrified and bowed with their faces to the ground. Then the men asked, "Why are you looking among the dead for someone who is alive? He isn't here! He is risen from the dead! Remember what he told you back in Galilee, that the Son of Man must be betrayed into the hands of sinful men and be crucified, and that he would rise again on the third day." Then they remembered that he had said this. So they rushed back from the tomb to tell his eleven disciples—and everyone else—what had happened. It was Mary Magdalene, Joanna, Mary the mother of James, and several other women who told the apostles what had happened.

LUKE 24:5–10

## Pray

*Lord let your Word be a light unto my path.*

## Observe

We often allow ourselves to worry unnecessarily. We grow anxious in the midst of our circumstances or troubled about completing our self-imposed chores and tasks. God calls us to set aside our anxiety and embrace his promises, peace, and protection. We can calm our fears by remembering and relying on God's Word.

In Matthew 6:25–34, Jesus reminds us to let go of worry, for worry can't "add a single moment to your life" (v. 27). He encourages us: "So don't worry about tomorrow, for tomorrow will bring its own worries. Today's trouble is enough for today" (v. 34).

Mary Magdalene and the other women with her were distraught over Jesus' death and disappearance. But the angels of the Lord questioned their concerns and told them to remember the words of Jesus. Then they embraced the truth, set aside their worries, and ran to tell others what had happened.

Courageously stop your worrying by implementing the following steps.

1. Give all your cares and concerns to the Lord in prayer (Philippians 4:6).
2. Search God's Word for verses that address your specific needs and commit them to memory (Proverbs 12:25).
3. Listen to worship music that brings comfort and encouragement to your heart and praise to your lips (Psalm 28:7).
4. Make a list of things you are anxious to accomplish and mark off ones that are unnecessary and not from God (Luke 10:41–42).

## Interpret

God expects us to remember his Word and allow it to calm our fears and direct our path in the midst of every life situation.

## Apply

Courageously let go of your worries and anxieties today and let God comfort your heart and give peace for your soul.

## Pray

*Father, I often get caught up in my to-do list and fail to eliminate needless tasks. Grant me peace of mind and give me the ability to eliminate unnecessary chores and trust you with all I have.*

# Day 56

# LET TRUTH COME ALIVE

## (LYDIA)

One of them was Lydia from Thyatira, a merchant of expensive
purple cloth, who worshiped God. As she listened to us,
the Lord opened her heart, and she accepted what Paul was
saying. She and her household were baptized and she asked
us to be her guests. "If you agree that I am a true believer in
the Lord," she said, "come and stay at my home." And she
urged us until we agreed. When Paul and Silas left the prison,
they returned to the home of Lydia. There they met with the
believers and encouraged them once more. Then they left
town.

ACTS 16:14–15, 40

## Pray

*Lord, pierce my heart and challenge my life as I
meditate on your Word.*

## Observe

God wants to walk with us and talk to us. Through
his Spirit and his Word, he gives us everything we need
to tackle every life situation. Scripture acts as a lamp
in our hand as we journey through this dark world of
endless choices.

As young Christians, we often don't realize that living within the cover of our practically untouched Bibles are life-giving words that provide comfort, inspiration, and knowledge of all things pertaining to God, life, and eternity. God's Word is alive and active, and as relevant today as it was the very first day it was penned.

God opened Lydia's heart, and she was so excited about the truth Paul shared that she insisted he and Silas stay at her home. She then opened her home as the first gathering place in Philippi where believers could be encouraged and taught.

Courageously allow God's Word to come alive by implementing the following practices:

1. Set aside a specific time and place to read God's Word for at least fifteen minutes a day.
2. Choose one book of the Bible and read one chapter each day until you complete the book.
3. Take notes on the truth you discover as you learn from God's Word.
4. Discuss what you've learned with a friend and ask them to join you in reading.

## Interpret

God's truth is alive and life-changing. When we take time to listen and learn from God and his Word, we can't help but share it with others.

## Apply

Choose a location in your home where you can quietly read God's Word and make a commitment to set aside fifteen minutes each day to read the Bible.

## Pray

*Father, your Word gives light and understanding. You wrote it for our instruction and encouragement. Please give me a passion for your Word and help me remain faithful in reading it each and every day.*

# OVERCOME ROADBLOCKS

## (CAROL M. SWAIN)

God says, "Rebuild the road! Clear away the rocks and stones so my people can return from captivity." The high and lofty one who lives in eternity, the Holy One, says this: "I live in the high and holy place with those whose spirits are contrite and humble. I restore the crushed spirit of the humble and revive the courage of those with repentant hearts."

ISAIAH 57:14–15

## *Pray*

*Lord, thank you for the remarkable gift of your Word. Help me to receive your truth.*

## *Observe*

Roadblocks restrict us from traveling in the direction we need to go. While external (or physical) roadblocks can be frustrating and inconvenient, the roadblocks that are especially destructive are the internal (or emotional) ones that hinder our personal and spiritual growth.

Internal roadblocks often delay us from moving forward; they cause us to be detoured or completely block our progress. They prevent us from accomplishing our objectives and ultimately keep us from reaching our God-given potential.

Christ purchased our freedom on the cross. Therefore we are commanded to stand firm in times of trial and embrace true freedom by letting go of the shame, self-condemnation, and lies we've embraced for so long.

Carol M. Swain grew up in poverty, dropped out of school in the ninth grade, and quickly became a mother of three children. As a single mom determined to support her young family, Carol overcame her lack of education by earning her GED and going on to eventually earn five college and university degrees. Today, she is a former professor at Vanderbilt University, a conservative television analyst, and an author of six books. Two associate justices of the United States Supreme Court have cited her scholarly work. Carol's passion is to empower others to also overcome their social, economic, and political barriers and inspire believers to stand up for our country's Judeo-Christian heritage.

Courageously overcome your roadblocks by putting the following principles into practice.

1. Pray and ask God to help you identify your roadblocks.

2. Openly admit the existence of your roadblocks.
3. Work to uncover the origin of your roadblocks.
4. Take the necessary steps to begin dismantling your roadblocks.

## Interpret

Christ died to set us free. Therefore God expects us to remove our roadblocks and no longer live in captivity.

## Apply

Pray and ask God to help you identify the roots of your roadblocks, share your findings with a godly friend or loved one today, and ask them to hold you accountable as you work to dismantle your obstacles.

## Pray

*Father, I am grateful that you desire to help me remove my roadblocks. Please give me the ability to identify and dismantle these obstacles so I can serve you with courage and in freedom.*

## Day 58

# LET GO OF YOUR PAST

### (WOMAN CAUGHT IN ADULTERY)

As he was speaking, the teachers of religious law and the
Pharisees brought a woman who had been caught in the act
of adultery. They put her in front of the crowd. "Teacher," they
said to Jesus, "this woman was caught in the act of adultery.
The law of Moses says to stone her. What do you say?" ... They
kept demanding an answer, so he stood up again and said,
"All right, but let the one who has never sinned throw the first
stone!" ... Then Jesus stood up again and said to the woman,
"Where are your accusers? Didn't even one of them condemn
you?" "No, Lord," she said. And Jesus said, "Neither do I. Go
and sin no more."

JOHN 8:3–5, 7, 10–11

*Pray*

Lord, show me how to handle my past with the
grace and forgiveness that comes from you.

*Observe*

Much too often, we struggle to overcome past pain,
bitterness, unforgiveness, and guilt. Without realizing
it, we allow former experiences to infect our attitudes,
personalities, relationships, and decisions.

God wants to free us from our slavery to fear, hurt, sin, or shame.

When Jesus was asked to condemn a woman who had been caught in adultery, he refused. He instead challenged her accusers to consider their sins and encouraged her to let go of her shame and sin no more.

Courageously let go of your past by completing the following exercise.

1. List areas of your life where fear, hurt, sin, and shame prevail.

2. Beside each occurrence, write the ways in which you attempt to cope with the inevitable pain.

3. Memorize the following passages and speak truth into your pain:
   - Second Timothy 1:7 (fear).
   - Psalm 147:3 (hurt).
   - First John 1:9 (sin).
   - Romans 8:1 (shame).

4. Pray and ask God to help you get to the root of your issues and discover proper ways to uproot your problems—once and for all.

## Interpret

There is no condemnation in Christ. Jesus wants us to embrace his forgiveness of our sins, as well as the sins of others. He wants us to put our sin and shame behind us and pursue righteousness.

## Apply

Are you holding on to past sin or shame in your life? Make a commitment today to receive Christ's forgiveness, let go of your past, and embrace the freedom Jesus paid for with his life.

## Pray

*Father, I am eternally thankful that you've cleansed me from past failures and sin the very moment I confessed and surrendered my life to you. Help me overcome my need to hold onto my past and give me the necessary courage to fully embrace your truth.*

# CHOOSE A POSITIVE PERSPECTIVE

## (ABIGAIL)

There was a wealthy man from Maon who owned property
near the town of Carmel. He had 3,000 sheep and 1,000
goats, and it was sheep-shearing time. This man's name was
Nabal, and his wife, Abigail, was a sensible and beautiful
woman. But Nabal, a descendant of Caleb, was crude and
mean in all his dealings.

1 Samuel 25:2–3

### Pray

*Lord, give me a deeper understanding of you and
your Word.*

### Observe

We all, at one time or another, find ourselves in
difficult relationships. Whether with a co-worker, boss,
friend, or family member, we often experience disputes
in relationships we wish were resolved. Too often, we
choose to avoid these challenging relationships rather
than addressing the issues at hand.

When we allow unresolved conflict to infect our
lives, it affects us spiritually, emotionally, and physically.
We can get so wrapped up in our disputes with others

that it distracts us from God's will for our lives and hinders our ability to pursue godly resolutions.

Jesus dealt with many difficult people during his lifetime, and he never hesitated to confront their dispute with truth in love. He will help us approach our difficult relationships with courage and confidence if we call on him to go with us and guide us.

Although Abigail lived with a drunken, angry, and evil man, she loved the Lord deeply. In spite of her heartbreaking relationship with her difficult husband, she kept a positive perspective and took the necessary steps to protect herself and her family.

In our pursuit of a godly life, we must wisely prepare and face our conflicts in Christ-like ways.

Courageously pursue a positive perspective in difficult relationships by implementing the following steps.

1. Carefully analyze all aspects of the issues within your relationships.
2. Take personal responsibility for your contribution to relational difficulties and accept the reality that you can't change other people.
3. Pray and prepare to confront each relational conflict in a godly way with courage and confidence.

4. Communicate care and speak truth in love to those with whom you are at odds. Ask forgiveness where you've been wrong, offer forgiveness to your offender, express love and concern for the relationship, and set healthy boundaries when necessary.

## Interpret

We can embrace a positive perspective and make godly decisions even when others around us are acting foolishly and unreasonably.

## Apply

Are you in a difficult relationship? Choose today to adopt a positive perspective and take one step toward addressing your conflict in a godly manner.

## Pray

*Father, help me to see my relationships the way you see them. Give me wisdom and discernment to approach relational issues with godly wisdom, clarity, courage, and unconditional love.*

## Day 60

# BE REFINED

### (MALALA YOUSAFZAI)

*"And I will bring the third part through the fire, Refine them as silver is refined, And test them as gold is tested. They will call on My name, and I will answer them; I will say, 'They are My people,' and they will say, 'The LORD is my God.'"*

ZECHARIAH 13:9 NASB

## Pray

Lord, help me to be a doer of your word and not just a hearer.

## Observe

Scripture compares God's purification of us to the purification of gold and silver. To remove impurities from gold or silver, you must heat them up to temperatures between 1,750 and 1,940 degrees Fahrenheit—extremely hot. While satan is the author of the adversities that burn us, God utilizes our suffering to cleanse us and mold us into the women he desires us to be.

As we go through painful experiences, it's important we ask God to reveal his intended lesson.

Instead of asking him to take away our trials, we are called to embrace them with courage and confidence. Remember, God sees within us great beauty and potential, and his desire is to cleanse us so we can become more like Christ.

Malala Yousafzai is the youngest person to ever receive the Nobel Peace Prize. After being shot in the head by a Taliban gunman in 2012 and having survived, her witness for Christ became louder and more courageous. Today she's a leading advocate for female rights and education in Pakistan. She founded the Malala Fund, which provides desperately needed education to young girls and contributes to positive changes within their families and communities.

Courageously allow God to refine you by embracing the following truths.

1. When troubles come your way, embrace them with joy, knowing when your life is tested, your endurance will grow (James 1:2–3).
2. When your faith is tested, adopt a positive outlook, knowing it honors God and great joy is ahead (1 Peter 1:6–7).
3. When you go through a trial, don't be surprised. You are partners in Christ's

suffering and will be rewarded when his
glory is revealed (1 Peter 4:12–13).

4. When you encounter life's
problems, know it will develop your
character and strengthen your hope in
salvation (Romans 5:3–5).

### Interpret

God often allows us to go through painful trials in
order to clean us up and bring us closer to him.

### Apply

Are you currently going through a painful trial?
Embrace your trial today as an opportunity to draw
closer to God and grow in faith.

### Pray

*Father, I know you see within me greater beauty
and potential. Please give me the courage to surrender
to your refining process and help me be transformed
into the person you desire for me to be.*

*Day 61*

# SURRENDER

## (SHIPHRAH AND PUAH)

Then Pharaoh, the king of Egypt, gave this order to the Hebrew
midwives, Shiphrah and Puah: "When you help the Hebrew
women as they give birth, watch as they deliver. If the baby
is a boy, kill him; if it is a girl, let her live."  But because the
midwives feared God, they refused to obey the king's orders.
They allowed the boys to live, too.

EXODUS 1:15–17

*Pray*

Lord, please give me wisdom as I approach your
Word.

*Observe*

Are you striving for something you just can't seem
to obtain or resisting something you just can't seem to
elude?

We often face situations that require our surrender,
yet we frequently struggle and strive to maintain control,
dogmatically standing firm in our own position no
matter how hard God tries to get our attention.

From the time we surrender our lives to Christ,

we are called to surrender to the guidance of the Holy Spirit—yet that often becomes one of our greatest struggles. Many of us spend years fighting against God's guidance in order to maintain the pursuit of our wants and ways. Until one day we see the cost of our battle and realize how we consistently complicate our lives.

Surrendering to God's will and way is a continual practice we must choose to make every day of our lives.

God calls each of us to surrender totally to him through his Son, Jesus Christ. So if we're ready for change—for forgiveness, peace, and limitless joy— then we must fully surrender to God and let him take complete control of our lives. Shiphrah and Puah were courageous believers in the one true God. They respectfully feared God more than man and were therefore prepared to surrender to God's will when Pharaoh ordered them to kill the Hebrew baby boys.

Courageously surrender to God's will by following these steps.

1. Begin each day by asking God for wisdom and guidance (James 1:5).
2. Memorize Romans 12:2 and make it a life verse.
3. Seek godly counsel regarding the direction of your life (Proverbs 19:20–21).

4. Lay aside your pride and place your complete trust in God's plans for your life (Jeremiah 29:11).

## Interpret

God expects his faithful followers to surrender to his will over the ungodly desires of the world.

## Apply

Is there an area in your life where you are struggling to surrender to God's will? What one step can you take today to deny the world's ways and embrace God's calling?

## Pray

*Father, help me to clearly see the worldly lies I am tempted to fall prey to. When I doubt my own ability, remind me of your promise to give me everything I need to accomplish your will.*

# GUARD YOUR HEART

(MARY, MOTHER OF JESUS)

Standing near the cross were Jesus' mother, and his mother's
sister, Mary (the wife of Clopas), and Mary Magdalene. When
Jesus saw his mother standing there beside the disciple he
loved, he said to her, "Dear woman, here is your son." And he
said to this disciple, "Here is your mother." And from then on
this disciple took her into his home.

JOHN 19:25–27

*Pray*

*Lord, let your Word be a light unto my path.*

*Observe*

Our ability to embrace joy comes from within and
not from our circumstances.

Have you ever taken inventory of what's at the
heart of your emotions? God gave us our feelings to
inform us of something deeper, something that has
either settled in our hearts or is on its way there. He
warns us to diligently watch over our hearts because
the matters of our hearts significantly impact our
everyday lives (Proverbs 4:23). Therefore, it's important
to regularly examine our hearts to discover negative

emotions that have settled there. We must manage our emotions—before they manage us.

When painful experiences occur, negative emotions arise. While it's normal to be sad, angry, embarrassed, or ashamed for a time, God doesn't want us to hold onto these feelings indefinitely. He wants us to process our pain and embrace healing for our emotions, so our joy can be restored.

When Mary brought her infant son Jesus into the Temple to be dedicated, Simeon embraced her baby, praised God for his glory, and warned Mary and Joseph that because of their son's destiny, a sword would pierce their very soul (Luke 2:33–35).

Mary experienced many painful life experiences, the most intense of which was witnessing her son being brutally beaten and crucified. But even as the sword pierced her heart, she remained patient and faithful and continued to trust God with every aspect of her life.

Courageously guard your heart by implementing the following steps.

1. Take inventory of any negative emotions you are experiencing.
2. Ask God to help you identify the painful event that initiated each negative emotion.
3. Pray for wisdom to work through your pain and heal your emotions.

4. Ask a godly friend to hold you accountable as you process your feelings and pain.

## Interpret

We all experience pain in our lives. God knows how we feel and will comfort us as we heal.

## Apply

Are you sad, angry, jealous, bitter, or struggling with unforgiveness? Name one step you can take today to begin the process of healing your negative emotions.

## Pray

*Father, you promise to never abandon us in our hour of need. Help me identify my heart issues and give me courage to take the necessary steps to heal my damaged emotions.*

*Day 63*

# SHARE YOUR STORY

## (KATHIE LEE GIFFORD)

Instead, you must worship Christ as Lord of your life. And if someone asks about your hope as a believer, always be ready to explain it. But do this in a gentle and respectful way.

1 PETER 3:15–16

*Pray*

Lord, give me a hunger for your Word and a desire to walk worthy of your calling.

*Observe*

People are waiting to be encouraged and inspired by our stories. We all love a good story. That's why we spend so much time reading books, watching television, and going to the movies. Stories inspire us and highlight life experiences we can relate to and learn from. They give us an opportunity to see life from another point of view.

One of the best ways to share the gospel of Christ is to share our personal testimonies. Yet many times we pass up opportunities because we lack courage and confidence. Our testimonies should be shared in conversational ways—in ways that engage our listeners, peak their interest, and keep them captivated. The best conversations consist of dialogue. Therefore, it's important for us to also keep our stories short and to the point, leaving plenty of time for questions and discussion.

When we share our testimonies for the first time, we sometimes stutter and stumble. But practice improves our delivery and enhances our likelihood of success.

Television host, singer, songwriter, actress, playwright, and author, Kathie Lee Gifford has always been willing to share her story. She openly acknowledges God's presence throughout her life and faithfully believes, "We are at our happiest in life when we're doing exactly what God created us to do." Kathie shared the gospel with over seventy million people when she spoke of her husband's passing and their faith in Christ.

Courageously share your salvation story with others by following these steps.

1. Briefly describe your life before Christ in one to two minutes.
2. Briefly describe how you came to know Christ in one to two minutes.
3. Briefly describe why you surrendered your life to Christ in one to two minutes.

4. Briefly describe how your life has changed after surrendering to Christ in one to two minutes.

## Interpret

God expects us to share our testimonies and lives with others so it will inspire and encourage their salvation and their walk with the Lord.

## Apply

Are you apprehensive about sharing your testimony? Set aside time today to write your salvation story and practice by sharing it with someone you know.

## Pray

*Father, I am so grateful for the way in which you've changed my life. Give me courage, confidence, and the opportunity to share my testimony with others so they too might experience true life-change.*

# Day 64

# TALK TO GOD

## (HANNAH)

Then Hannah prayed: "My heart rejoices in the LORD!
The LORD has made me strong. Now I have an answer for my
enemies; I rejoice because you rescued me. No one is holy
like the LORD! There is no one besides you; there is no Rock
like our God."

1 SAMUEL 2:1–2

## Pray

*Lord, let your Word be a mirror into my soul.*

## Observe

Jesus' life was saturated in prayer. It was vital to his
life and ministry, just as it is to ours. Prayer is the breath
of our spiritual life. God wants a close and personal
relationship with us, and he wants us to talk to him.

But we have a deterrent, one who wants to keep us
from communicating with God. Satan knows he will be
defeated through the power of our prayers, so he will do
everything he can to discourage us in our prayer life.

God's Word teaches us to have a prayer life
grounded in the simplicity of expression, sincerity of

heart, and trust in God's promises. Our prayers should center on God's will, his glory, his kingdom, as well as our need for intervention, support, and deliverance. It's vital we set aside time each day for prayer. Keep it simple, pray over every situation, and always give thanks.

Hannah talked to God through her prayers; she knew where her strength came from, and she rejoiced in her relationship with God. She faithfully prayed and turned to the Lord for encouragement when she was deeply hurt and ridiculed by Peninnah (1:7).

Communication with God is a gift—one we should not take for granted.

Courageously communicate with God each day by implementing the following practices when you pray.

1. Begin by acknowledging God's majesty and sovereign power (Proverbs 3:6).
2. Give thanks for everything God provides in your life (Psalm 100:4).
3. Draw near to God with confidence, knowing he hears your requests (1 John 5:14).
4. Pray without ceasing, at all times, in all places, and during all circumstances (1 Thessalonians 5:16–18).

## Interpret

God's followers are to talk to God through their prayers. Our prayers should acknowledge gratitude and praise for who God is, what he has done, and how his children can rely on him to provide for their every need.

## Apply

How often do you talk to God? Do you talk to him multiple times each day? Take time today to thank God for his continual presence.

## Pray

*Father, I am eternally grateful for your love and willingness to hear my prayers and care for my concerns. Give me courage today to leave my cares and concerns with you—the one who knows best how to direct my path and restore my soul.*

# PLEDGE TO PERSEVERE

## (ABIJAH)

Hezekiah son of Ahaz began to rule over Judah in the third
year of King Hoshea's reign in Israel. He was twenty-five
years old when he became king, and he reigned in Jerusalem
twenty-nine years. His mother was Abijah, the daughter of
Zechariah. He did what was pleasing in the Lord's sight, just
as his ancestor David had done.

2 Kings 18:1–3

## Pray

*Lord, help me develop a deeper desire for you as I
encounter your Word.*

## Observe

Perseverance is a quality we must strive to obtain,
strengthen, and exercise throughout life. When facing a
challenge, setback, or failure, perseverance gives us the
ability to push through our difficulty and continue moving
forward toward a more prosperous and productive future.

We all experience trials in life, some
manageable—some not so much. The important thing
to remember is that we must strive to persevere through
each and every challenge and trust God's sovereign will

to be done in the end. God's Word promotes endurance and supplies encouragement both through instruction and by example. "For whatever was written in earlier times was written for our instruction, so that through perseverance and the encouragement of the Scriptures we might have hope" (Romans 15:4 NASB).

Through the perseverance of others, we draw strength. Throughout the Bible, we read accounts of others who have persevered, inspiring us to do the same. Abijah was the mother of Hezekiah and the wife of King Ahaz. It is evident by the life of her son, who was a godly king, that she persevered in her faith and taught her son to do so as well, in spite of being married to an evil king who worshiped pagan gods and even sacrificed his own son (1 Kings 16:3).

Courageously persevere by exercising the following practices.

1. Seek courage, guidance, and strength from God.
2. Allow the perseverance of Christ to inspire you to endure your hardships.
3. Be encouraged by the accounts of others who have persevered through their trials.
4. Memorize James 1:2–3 and allow this verse to encourage you in your spiritual walk with God.

## Interpret

We must choose to persevere in our faith and faithfulness, regardless of our circumstances or the influences of others.

## Apply

Do you find it difficult to persevere in your faith or faithfulness? Name someone in your life who has persevered through a challenging experience. Be inspired by that person's persistence and determination and make a commitment today to persevere through your own trials.

## Pray

*Father, I am thankful that you give me everything I need to endure hardships. Help me run the race you have set before me with courage and perseverance, keeping my eyes on Jesus, the author and perfector of my faith.*

# OVERCOME OPPOSITION

## (GLADYS AYLWARD)

I pray that God, the source of hope, will fill you completely with
joy and peace because you trust in him. Then you will overflow
with confident hope through the power of the Holy Spirit.

ROMANS 15:13

## Pray

Lord, align my heart with your precepts contained
in your Word.

## Observe

There are times in life when we are overwhelmed,
under pressure, and face opposition. In times like these,
we must learn to turn solely to Jesus, our never-ending
source of wisdom, strength, hope, and help. In doing so,
we will experience firsthand the overwhelming presence
of God in the midst of our circumstances. When we
stop listening to the naysayers and allow God's voice to
reign, we will stand firm, overcome our obstacles, and
ultimately accomplish God's will for our lives.

When God's people are determined to do God's
will, future generations benefit, lives are transformed,

hearts are changed, and souls are saved. Truly, all things are possible with God, if we embrace our God-given courage and go after our God-given dreams.

Gladys Aylward had a dream of going to China to become a missionary, but she lived during a time and in a country where women primarily served as teachers and nurses. So without support from a mission board, she took her life savings and bought a one-way ticket to Yangcheng, Shanxi Province, China.

In order to support herself, Gladys became a foot inspector for the Chinese government, helping officials enforce their ban against binding the feet of little girls. Her work led her to minister to orphans. Gladys has been honored and recognized for her efforts in protecting the children in China from the Japanese invasion. Time after time, God helped Gladys triumph over impossible situations and through her, drew people to Himself.

Courageously overcome your opposition and pursue God's calling by implementing the following principles.

1. Focus on the power of God rather than the opposition of this world.
2. Tune out the voices of discouragement and listen consistently to God's encouragement.

3. Be obedient to God and his Word
   in order to eliminate distractions and
   detours.
4. Ask godly friends and loved ones
   to pray for you as you pursue God's will.

## Interpret

When we fully trust God, he will completely fill us with joy, peace, and confident hope through the power of the Holy Spirit.

## Apply

Is there something standing in your way of following God's call on your life? Take at least one step today toward overcoming your obstacles and pursue your God-given dreams with passion.

## Pray

*Father, thank you for being my constant source of hope, courage, and passion. Give me the ability to accomplish your will and help me overcome the obstacles that aim to discourage me.*

# LET YOUR LIGHT SHINE

## (DORCAS/TABITHA)

There was a believer in Joppa named Tabitha (which in Greek is Dorcas). She was always doing kind things for others and helping the poor. About this time she became ill and died. Her body was washed for burial and laid in an upstairs room. But the believers had heard that Peter was nearby at Lydda, so they sent two men to beg him, "Please come as soon as possible!"

ACTS 9:36–38

*Pray*

*Lord, help me to be a doer of your Word and not just a hearer.*

*Observe*

Have you ever wondered how the term "Christian" came into being—what it meant during the culture of the early church versus what it means in our culture today?

Throughout the Gospels, we read numerous accounts of Christ displaying his identity rather than merely telling followers "who he is." In Acts 11:26 we find that "the disciples were first called Christians in Antioch" (NASB). The term "Christian" only occurs in three verses throughout the entire Bible—each time by outsiders, referring to Christ-followers and not by Christians referring to themselves. Being a "Christian" has much more to do with how we act and how others perceive us, rather than how we perceive ourselves.

It's important we always stand up, speak up, and proclaim our allegiance to Christ with courage and confidence, while outwardly displaying behavior in keeping with the character of Christ.

Dorcas let others see her faith through her actions and behaviors; she was known for her kindness and assistance to the poor. She was loved so much by the people in her community that when she died, her "room was filled with widows who were weeping and showing the coats and other clothes Dorcas had made for them" (Acts 9:39).

Courageously express your faith in Christ by letting your actions speak and ask yourself the following questions.

1. Do I allow God to fully work in and through me?
2. Am I letting my faith in Christ shine or do I keep it hidden?
3. How often do I express my dedication to God through my actions?

4. If asked, who would others say I am? Would they quickly acknowledge my Christian faith?

## Interpret

God wants us to live out our faith so others will see our love for him expressed through our attitudes, choices, and actions.

## Apply

Show your love for God today by doing something kind for a stranger.

## Pray

*Father, I want you to work in and through me every day, and I want others to recognize my love and dedication to you. Please give me the courage to let my light shine before others so they may see your great works and glorify your holy name.*

# CONFRONT CONFLICT

## (ZELOPHEHAD'S DAUGHTERS)

One day a petition was presented by the daughters of
Zelophehad—Mahlah, Noah, Hoglah, Milcah, and Tirzah.
Their father, Zelophehad, was a descendant of Hepher son
of Gilead, son of Makir, son of Manasseh, son of Joseph.
These women stood before Moses, Eleazar the priest, the
tribal leaders, and the entire community at the entrance of
the Tabernacle. "Our father died in the wilderness," they said.
"He was not among Korah's followers, who rebelled against
the LORD; he died because of his own sin. But he had no sons.
Why should the name of our father disappear from his clan
just because he had no sons? Give us property along with the
rest of our relatives."

NUMBERS 27:1–4

## Pray

*Lord, give me focus and direction as I study your
Word.*

## Observe

There are times when God calls us to stand up
for ourselves and courageously confront conflict in an
honest and honorable way.

At one time or another, we all find ourselves in difficult situations or relationships. Jesus dealt with many difficult people during his lifetime, yet he never hesitated to face each conflict with truth in love. If we want to be more like Christ, we must be willing to face conflict.

Zelophehad's daughters didn't hesitate to face their conflict in a godly way. They courageously stood before Moses to defend their rights. As a result of their courage, their legitimate claim acknowledged by God was honored by Moses, and a new rule was put in place for God's people (Numbers 27:7–8).

Courageously confront conflict by implementing the following steps.

1. **Pray**. Ask God for guidance as you prepare to confront your conflict. Pray for courage and ask God to help you use the right words and have the right attitude.
2. **Prepare**. Prepare mentally to face your conflict with courage. Ask a godly friend to listen objectively and give you godly advice. Ask them to help you prepare to speak truth, to ask for forgiveness, and to forgive.
3. **Plan**. Determine a godly way to confront your dispute and set a time and place to meet.

4. **Persevere**. Relational conflict is never easy. Regardless, it's something we must courageously face, even when we simply don't feel like it.

## Interpret

Blessings come to those who are willing to stand up for what's right in the eyes of God.

## Apply

Is God calling you to confront a legitimate dispute in your life? Ask God for guidance and the courage to take at least one step today to face your challenge.

## Pray

*Father, thank you for giving me the encouragement to confront my conflict. Help me respond with humility, honesty, and courage to stand firm in truth as I face any opposition.*

# BELIEVE GOD

## (SOJOURNER TRUTH)

And it is impossible to please God without faith. Anyone who wants to come to him must believe that God exists and that he rewards those who sincerely seek him.

HEBREWS 11:6

## Pray

Lord, open my mind to the Spirit of Truth as I read and study your Word.

## Observe

When we believe God, we open up endless possibilities. But when we rely on our own strength, we fall into emotional self-traps that limit our progress and keep us from pursuing opportunities outside our comfort zone. Destructive self-traps limit our ability to make God-honoring decisions.

There are four destructive self-traps we often get caught in: selfishness, self-sufficiency, self-condemnation, and self-protectiveness. The selfish person says, "I will take what I want and do what I want." The self-sufficient person says, "I don't need any help; I can take care of myself." The self-condemning person says, "I'm not good enough to do what needs to be done." The self-protective person says, "I must be very careful, otherwise I'll get hurt."

Isabella Baumfree was born into slavery in Swartwkill, New York. In 1826, she took her infant daughter and escaped to freedom and soon became an outspoken opponent of slavery and an activist for women's rights. She sensed God calling her to travel throughout the United States to share her testimony and present the gospel. Out of fear for her life, her children discouraged her from pursuing her dream. But Isabella, who adopted the name Sojourner Truth, reassured her family that if God was calling her, as she genuinely believed, he would surely protect her.

Courageously believe God and avoid self-traps by meditating on the following verses.

1. **Avoid selfishness**: "Do not merely look out for your own personal interests, but also for the interests of others" (Philippians 2:4 NASB).

2. **Avoid self-sufficiency**: "Two people are better off than one, for they can help each other succeed" (Ecclesiastes 4:9).

3. **Avoid self-condemnation**: "Therefore there is now no condemnation

for those who are in Christ Jesus" (Romans
8:1 NASB).

4. **Avoid self-protectiveness**: "Be strong and
courageous, do not be afraid or tremble
at them, for the LORD your God is the one
who goes with you. He will not fail you or
forsake you" (Deuteronomy 31:6 NASB).

## Interpret

When we believe in God and have unwavering
faith in his ability, we can please him and receive our
reward.

## Apply

Do you believe God, or are you more apt to rely
on your own abilities and strengths? Determine your
self-trap and share your realization with a godly friend
or loved one today.

## Pray

*Father, thank you for being patient with me as I
strive to trust you with my future. Help me clearly see
the direction you want me to go and give me courage
and reassurance as you see me through.*

# ASK FORGIVENESS

## (HULDAH)

So Hilkiah and the other men went to the New Quarter of
Jerusalem to consult with the prophet Huldah. She was the wife
of Shallum son of Tikvah, son of Harhas, the keeper of the Temple
wardrobe. She said to them, "The LORD, the God of Israel, has
spoken! Go back and tell the man who sent you, 'This is what the
LORD says: I am going to bring disaster on this city and its people.
All the curses written in the scroll that was read to the king of
Judah will come true.' ... "But go to the king of Judah who sent
you to seek the LORD and tell him: 'This is what the LORD, the God
of Israel, says concerning the message you have just heard: You
were sorry and humbled yourself before God when you heard his
words against this city and its people. You humbled yourself and
tore your clothing in despair and wept before me in repentance.
And I have indeed heard you, says the LORD.'"

2 CHRONICLES 34:22–24, 26–27

## Pray

Lord, unlock the mysteries of your Word that I
might know your will.

## Observe

Anyone can say "I'm sorry," but it takes courage to
truly repent.

To avoid conflict and to keep the peace, we often apologize without really being remorseful. As we mature in our relationship with the Lord, we begin to realize there is a big difference between simply voicing, "I'm sorry" and genuinely admitting, "I am wrong … will you forgive me?"

When King Hilkiah and his men approached the prophetess Huldah, she spoke God's Word to them and told them that Judah would be spared from the coming judgment during King Josiah's lifetime because of his humility and sincere repentance.

Courageously ask God and others for forgiveness by exercising these steps.

1. Praise God for his consistent character and willingness to forgive your sins.
2. Approach God and others you've sinned against with a humble and repentant heart.
3. Confess your sins and wrongdoings to God and others.
4. Ask God and those you've sinned against for their grace-filled forgiveness.

## Interpret

God relents on his judgment when his children confess their sins, humble themselves, and ask for forgiveness.

## Apply

Take time today to confess your sins to God. Then confront those you've hurt, genuinely ask for forgiveness, and vow to change your behavior.

## Pray

*Father, when I confess my sins, you are faithful to forgive me and cleanse me from all unrighteousness. Thank you for your mercy and grace. Please give me courage to be honest with others and myself and help me ask for forgiveness in ways that genuinely express my true remorse.*

# EMBRACE YOUR CALLING

## (ELISABETH)

When Herod was king of Judea, there was a Jewish priest named
Zechariah. He was a member of the priestly order of Abijah,
and his wife, Elizabeth, was also from the priestly line of Aaron.
Zechariah and Elizabeth were righteous in God's eyes, careful to
obey all of the Lord's commandments and regulations.

LUKE 1:5–6

*Pray*

   *Lord, give me the ability to see the wondrous truth
in your Word.*

*Observe*

   What does it mean to be called? How can we truly
discern God's calling on our lives?

   The more we grow in our faith and understanding of
God, the easier it will be to recognize God's voice. One
of the first places we can look for God's voice is in his
Word. God speaks to us through his Spirit, and he speaks
to us through his Word. As children of God, we are called
by his Spirit to turn away from our sin and go deeper in
our relationship with him. Commonly, God's calling is

described as a burning desire that cannot be quenched—one that you cannot help but recognize and surrender to.

Sometimes God will lead us into unexpected places, way outside of our comfort zone—where he alone can help us accomplish his will. Our job is to be ready and willing to say yes anytime God communicates his call.

Elisabeth and her husband Zacharias were faithful followers of God. They were ready and willing to answer God's call, even when it meant they would birth and raise a son in their later years of life. Elisabeth was eager to embrace her calling, and she became the mother of John the Baptist, the man who would prepare God's people for the coming of the Lord (Luke 1:17).

As believers, we are all individually gifted and called according to God's purpose (Romans 8:28–30).

Courageously embrace your calling by answering the following questions.

1. Do I sense a calling on my life today?
2. Does it line up with the Word of God?
3. What steps can I take to pursue my calling?
4. Will I answer God's call right away?

## Interpret

God calls his followers to live righteously and ready to courageously embrace his calling on their lives—no matter how unique or unexpected one's calling may be.

## Apply

Take five minutes to pray. Ask God to clearly reveal his calling on your life. Take another five minutes to quietly listen, then write down what you sense God is saying.

## Pray

*Father, you've designed me to be unique and you've gifted me in ways I may not even realize. Help me to recognize your calling and give me a burning desire to faithfully pursue your will for my life.*

# ANALYZE YOUR ATTITUDE

## (NIKKI HALEY)

Do everything without complaining and arguing, so that no one can criticize you. Live clean, innocent lives as children of God, shining like bright lights in a world full of crooked and perverse people.

PHILIPPIANS 2:14–15

## *Pray*

*Lord, through the power of your Holy Spirit reveal your truth to me.*

## *Observe*

Our attitude can be defined as what we choose to do with our thoughts and feelings. They can range from positive to negative and anywhere in between. And they are a primary factor in our lives and relationships.

Our attitudes have a profound impact on our outcomes and overall health. When an event happens—feelings arise. Out of our feelings, we develop a particular way of thinking. How we allow ourselves to think impacts the attitude we adopt. Therefore, the more control we have over our thoughts and feelings, the more control we have over our attitudes.

In Philippians 2, Paul focuses on the attitude of believers, urging them to have the same attitude that is in Christ—one of encouragement, love, affection, compassion, unselfishness, and humility; not only looking out for our personal interests, but also the interests of others (2:1–4).

United States Ambassador Nikki R. Haley is a great example of someone who courageously maintains a respectful attitude in the midst of some challenging circumstances. The daughter of Indian immigrants, Nikki became the first Indian-American governor and the first female governor of South Carolina. Haley has been described as smart and savvy, and she has faced a considerable amount of public scrutiny for her positions.

Courageously analyze your attitudes and exchange your negative ones for ones modeled by Christ.

1. Make a list of any negative attitudes you need to change on an index card.
2. Write Philippians 2:1–5 on the other side of your card; read your card and memorize this passage.
3. Spend time in prayer asking God to heal your negative attitude and replace it with the attitude of Christ.
4. When you catch yourself falling into the trap of a negative attitude,

recall Philippians 2:1–5 and commit to
exchanging it for the attitude of Christ.

## Interpret

God commands us to have a good attitude and
live a clean life so we can represent him well and avoid
legitimate criticism from the world.

## Apply

Analyze your attitude today and ask God to help
you eliminate any tendency you have to be negative.

## Pray

*Father, I am grateful you are patient with me and
give me an abundance of second chances. Please help
me recognize my bad attitudes and give me the ability
to overcome them and pursue attitudes that honor you.*

# BE GENEROUS

## (THE WIDOW'S MITE)

While Jesus was in the Temple, he watched the rich people dropping their gifts in the collection box. Then a poor widow came by and dropped in two small coins. "I tell you the truth," Jesus said, "this poor widow has given more than all the rest of them. For they have given a tiny part of their surplus, but she, poor as she is, has given everything she has."

LUKE 21:1–4

## Pray

*Lord, align my heart with your generosity.*

## Observe

Generosity is not just about what we give—but also how we give. God loves a generous giver (2 Corinthians 9:7). When we give intentionally, generously, and joyfully, it is an expression of our gratitude and faith in the one who generously gave his life for us. After all, Christ displayed the ultimate expression of generosity when he gave his life for our salvation—the least we can do is celebrate his gift by giving to others.

One evidence of the depth in which the gospel has

penetrated our soul is expressed through our generosity. When God calls us to be generous, he isn't simply referring to our finances. God calls us to be charitable with our time and talents as well. Time is something we all have, but we are called to spend it wisely and use some of it to benefit others. We have all been given unique abilities and talents that can be used to generously serve others.

Never forget: you can't out-give God.

In Luke 21:1–4 and Mark 12:41–43, Jesus refers to the generosity of a widow. Others came into the Temple and gave a portion of their surplus, but the widow gave everything she had—two very small copper coins. Proportionate to her financial worth, the widow's gift was far more valuable than the gifts of the wealthy.

Be a courageous giver by practicing the following.

1. Be consistent in tithing ten percent of your income.
2. Pray and ask God for discernment regarding what he wants you to give above your tithe.
3. Give of your time to encourage, care for, and help those in need.
4. Use your God-given talents to meet the needs of others.

## Interpret

Jesus is pleased when we give generously and joyfully.

## Apply

Name at least one person you know who is in need and one way you can specifically help meet his or her need today.

## Pray

*Father, give me your eyes that I might clearly see the needs of others and help me to know the ways you desire for me to become a more generous giver.*

*Day 74*

# PREPARE FOR BATTLE

## (DEBORAH)

Deborah, the wife of Lappidoth, was a prophet who was judging Israel at that time. … One day she sent for Barak son of Abinoam, who lived in Kedesh in the land of Naphtali. She said to him, "This is what the LORD, the God of Israel, commands you: Call out 10,000 warriors from the tribes of Naphtali and Zebulun at Mount Tabor. And I will call out Sisera, commander of Jabin's army, along with his chariots and warriors, to the Kishon River. There I will give you victory over him."

JUDGES 4:4, 6–7

*Pray*

*Lord, help me to hunger and thirst for your promises found in your Word.*

*Observe*

Could it be the biggest issues in our marriages, families, workplaces, and churches are not other people—but the devil himself? Quite often, people aren't the real problem—they're simply victims of our true enemy—satan.

Through the prophetess and Judge Deborah, God commanded the Israelites to prepare for battle.

In courageous faith and obedience, Deborah, her commander, and the Israelite army headed into battle. God threw the Canaanite army into a panic and secured Israel's victory over their ruthless oppressors (Judges 4:14–15).

In the same way God called Israel to prepare for battle, God calls us to prepare to stand firm against our spiritual adversary—satan (Ephesians 6:11-12).

Courageously prepare for battle daily by putting on the Armor of God (Ephesians 6:10–18).

1. Wear the *Belt of Truth* and allow God's Truth to hold you up.
2. Guard your heart with the *Breastplate of Righteousness* and let Christ-like character be your heart's desire.
3. Prepare your feet with the *Gospel of Peace* and be God's messenger bringing good news to the wounded.
4. Take up the *Shield of Faith* and join other faithful warriors in deflecting satan's attacks.
5. Put on the *Helmet of Salvation* and protect your mind and thoughts from deception.
6. Embrace the *Sword of the Spirit,* which is the Word of God, and allow the power of God's Word to prevail over satan's lies.
7. *Pray at all times,* being completely alert and prepared for any and all battles.

## Interpret

God commands us to prepare for battle against our enemy, satan, and God promises to go before us to secure our victory.

## Apply

Are you prepared for spiritual attacks from satan? Review each piece of God's armor and make a commitment today to strengthen at least one area of your armor that is weak.

## Pray

*Father, I am grateful you supply me with everything I need to withstand spiritual attacks. Help me identify parts of my armor that are weak and give me courage to strengthen each area that's vulnerable.*

# CONSIDER MISSIONS

## (LOTTIE MOON)

Jesus came and told his disciples, "I have been given all
authority in heaven and on earth. Therefore, go and make
disciples of all the nations, baptizing them in the name of
the Father and the Son and the Holy Spirit. Teach these new
disciples to obey all the commands I have given you. And be
sure of this: I am with you always, even to the end of the age."

MATTHEW 28:18–20

*Pray*

*Lord, prepare my heart and mind and give me a
teachable spirit.*

*Observe*

As believers and disciples of Christ, the first and
most important reason we do mission work is to carry
the message of the gospel forward.

Christ made it clear to those whom he had
instructed that they were to go and make disciples of
others. Just as Christ's first disciples were to train new
disciples, we too, as followers of Christ, are commanded
to go and make disciples: a repetitive pattern that

ultimately achieves Christ's commanded goal—"make disciples of all nations" (v. 19).

If we are to be obedient to Christ, we must implement the necessary components of discipleship every chance we get—whether abroad, or right next door in our own communities. Discipleship, as illustrated by Christ and his disciples, consisted of four primary components: teaching God's Word, developing relationships, ministering to the needs of others, and training future teachers.

Teacher and evangelist Charlotte 'Lottie' Moon spent nearly forty years in China as a Southern Baptist missionary. She shared the gospel throughout villages and started schools. Lottie was concerned about the conditions for missionaries, so she laid the groundwork for what today is "the largest, single missionary offering among Baptists in America," the Lottie Moon Christmas Offering.

Courageously consider your mission as a disciple of Christ by adopting the following truths.

1. You are to sow God's word, realizing some will hear, accept, and bear fruit, while others will fall away (Mark 4:14–20).
2. You are to develop and nurture relationships by spending quality time with others (John 3:22).

3. You are to minister to others by
   caring for their needs (Matthew 25:35–40).
4. You are to help train future leaders by
   teaching them to teach others (Luke 6:40).

## Interpret

God helps us succeed in our mission. We are commanded to make disciples, teaching others to obey God's commands and become disciple-makers themselves.

## Apply

What are you currently doing to fulfill God's great commission of discipleship? Ask God what step he would have you take today and take it.

## Pray

*Father, help me understand my responsibility to support missions and make disciples. Give me wisdom and discernment and help me take the necessary steps to be obedient to you and your Word.*

# COUNT YOUR BLESSINGS

## (NAOMI)

So Ruth gathered barley there all day, and when she beat out
the grain that evening, it filled an entire basket. She carried
it back into town and showed it to her mother-in-law. Ruth
also gave her the roasted grain that was left over from her
meal. "Where did you gather all this grain today?" Naomi
asked. "Where did you work? May the Lord bless the one who
helped you!" So Ruth told her mother-in-law about the man
in whose field she had worked. She said, "The man I worked
with today is named Boaz." "May the Lord bless him!" Naomi
told her daughter-in-law. "He is showing his kindness to us as
well as to your dead husband. That man is one of our closest
relatives, one of our family redeemers."

RUTH 2:17–20

*Pray*

*Lord, let me clearly observe truth in your Word and
properly apply it to my life.*

*Observe*

We can get so caught up in worrying about what's
wrong in our lives that we neglect to appreciate what's
*right*. It's easy to be distracted by the busyness of life and
take for granted the many blessings that surround us.

We all have hardships, but we also have blessings to be thankful for. If we think about it, there are many people, places, and things we can be grateful for; things others are likely praying for right now.

After Naomi's husband and sons died, she returned to Bethlehem to seek help from relatives. Preoccupied with her pain and suffering, Naomi returned to her native land broken, hopeless, and convinced God had abandoned her. Over time, she began to embrace new hope and recognized the gift God had given her through her faithful and sacrificial daughter-in-law.

Courageously count your blessings by implementing the following steps.

1. Ask yourself: "What am I grateful for, and what am I taking for granted?"
2. Write down ten things you are thankful for and pray over each one.
3. Name at least one person you are thankful for and reach out to let that person know.
4. Thank God for your blessings and allow them to be the focus of your day.

## Interpret

God sends help in times of suffering. It's up to us to recognize his favor and count our blessings.

## Apply

Adopt an attitude of gratitude today that will brighten your personality, outlook, performance, and relationships.

## Pray

*Father, this is the day you have made. I will rejoice and be glad in it. Everything I have is a gift from you. Help me focus on the blessings you have given me and not the problems of life that seek to distract me.*

# RECOGNIZE OPPORTUNITIES

## (ESTHER)

Mordecai sent this reply to Esther: "Don't think for a moment that because you're in the palace you will escape when all other Jews are killed. If you keep quiet at a time like this, deliverance and relief for the Jews will arise from some other place, but you and your relatives will die. Who knows if perhaps you were made queen for just such a time as this?"

ESTHER 4:13–14

*Pray*

Lord, align my heart with your precepts contained in your Word.

*Observe*

Has God put you in a relationship, job, or circumstance for such a time as this?

Courage is being willing to pursue God-given opportunities in spite of danger or difficulty. It helps us to face challenging circumstances and allows us to make prudent choices, even when they are unpopular. It takes courage to embrace our God-given calling.

Fear, on the other hand, can be paralyzing. It can

cause us to remain in unhealthy relationships, make unhealthy choices, and keep us from embracing the possibilities.

We are all given countless opportunities to achieve our God-given potential, but we must seize them immediately before they disappear. Open doors don't remain open indefinitely. God can and will pass us by if we fail to recognize or heed his calling. If we sit idly by waiting for everything to be "right," we will miss our chance to embrace God's assignment.

In the book of Esther, we read the account of a young woman who, in God's providence, won the heart of a Persian king so she would be instrumentally positioned to influence the reversal of a decree that called for the massacre of the Jews.

Courageously recognize and seize your God-given opportunities by following these principles.

1. Ask God to help you recognize the assignments he has for you.
2. Pay attention to the Holy Spirit's prompting.
3. Replace negative self-talk with positive statements like: "With God all things are possible," "I can do this with God's help," "This opportunity is worth taking risks."

4. Be ready and willing to take action—don't procrastinate.

## Interpret

God often puts us in situations and places for a particular assignment. God knows all things and holds the past, present, and future securely in his hands.

## Apply

Where has God placed you in order to achieve his will? Are you in a relationship, job, or circumstance where you sense God encouraging you to exercise your faith and faithfulness? Make a commitment today to seize your God-given opportunity and take the first step to pursue his will.

## Pray

*Father, you know all things past, present, and future—you're already there. Help me recognize your calling and give me the courage and ability to carry out your will.*

# HONOR GOD

## (ROMA DOWNEY)

Don't you realize that your body is the temple of the Holy Spirit, who lives in you and was given to you by God? You do not belong to yourself, for God bought you with a high price. So you must honor God with your body.

1 Corinthians 6:19–20

### Pray

*Lord, help me embrace all you teach me as I meditate on your Word.*

### Observe

As Christians, we must realize our lives were bought at a price and they now belong to God. Therefore, we are to honor him in all our ways—our thoughts, actions, beliefs, and behaviors.

We honor God by being honest about our struggles and shortcomings. God is a God of mercy and grace, and the Christian life is a life of repentance and second chances. The world needs to see real people with real problems who are loved unconditionally and cared for by God. When we attempt to display perfection, we dishonor God; we place him out of reach for the unbelieving sinner, and we set ourselves up for failure and hypocrisy.

To bring glory to God requires pure motives and a good attitude. No matter what we do or where we are, we can honor God by how we present ourselves, how we treat others, and how we exemplify our devotion and dedication to our Savior.

Roma Downey is an Emmy-nominated actress, successful producer, and faithful Christian. She and her husband, Mark Burnett, have produced a faith-based movie and multiple biblically based television series. Roma has been named as one of the "100 Most Powerful Women in Hollywood." It has been said that one of Roma's greatest strengths is the grace she brings to every negotiation, development, and production. In her own words, she has said, "If I were to look back at my career, I think my greatest achievement is very simple. I've been able to make choices where I could glorify God."

Courageously honor God by living by the following truths.

1. Honor God by obeying his commandments (John 14:15).
2. Honor God through your praise and worship (Psalm 29:1–2).

3. Honor God by making his name famous (Psalm 105:1).
4. Honor God through your generosity toward others (2 Corinthians 9:13).

## Interpret

As Christians, we are to live in light of the fact that Christ bought us with a price. Therefore, we are to honor him with our bodies and our lives.

## Apply

Name one change you can make in your life today to honor God with your body and take the first step in making that change.

## Pray

*Father, I am forever grateful for your sacrifice that paid my sin debt in full. Please help me faithfully honor you in everything I do.*

# DEFEND THE DEFENSELESS

## (JEHOSHEBA)

When Athaliah, the mother of King Ahaziah of Judah, learned that her son was dead, she began to destroy the rest of the royal family. But Ahaziah's sister Jehosheba, the daughter of King Jehoram, took Ahaziah's infant son, Joash, and stole him away from among the rest of the king's children, who were about to be killed. She put Joash and his nurse in a bedroom, and they hid from Athaliah, so the child was not murdered. Joash remained hidden in the Temple of the LORD for six years while Athaliah ruled over the land.

2 KINGS 11:1–3

*Pray*

*Lord, open my mind to the Spirit of Truth as I read and study your Word.*

*Observe*

God's Word tells us to not only look out for our interests, but also the interests of others (Philippians 2:4), to give and we will receive (Luke 6:38), and to share one another's burdens and thereby fulfill the law of Christ (Galatians 6:2).

Although everyone may not be able to bring an orphan into their home or physically care for the needs of a homeless man, woman, or child, some can, and others can provide badly needed resources and funding to make their care possible.

Many times, we allow our busy lives to hinder our ability to recognize the distress of others. How often does a boss walk by an employee and ask, "How are you today?" Only to keep on walking in hopes he or she will give the customary response, "I'm fine—and you?" Do we really care about how others are doing? And when we're made aware of their needs, how willing are we to jump in and help?

Jehosheba, the King of Judah's aunt, courageously protected her nephew from his murderous mother and, as a result, preserved the lineage of Judah.

Courageously help the helpless by participating in one or more of the following practices.

1. Help connect a person in need with a ministry or agency.
2. Spend quality time with someone in need.
3. Volunteer at an organization that serves people in need.
4. Donate goods or funds to ministries and organizations that meet people's needs.

## Interpret

God commands his people to love and care for one another. He reminds believers that when they provide for the needs of their brothers and sisters, they are actually giving to the Lord (Matthew 25:35).

## Apply

Ask God to bring to your mind someone in need of your help. Then find ways today to help care for this person's needs.

## Pray

*Father, give me your eyes of compassion that I might clearly see those around me in need. Help me love unconditionally, give selflessly, and embrace a desire to make a difference.*

# SET HEALTHY BOUNDARIES

## (MICHAL)

When Saul realized that the LORD was with David and how much his daughter Michal loved him, Saul became even more afraid of him, and he remained David's enemy for the rest of his life. … Then Saul sent troops to watch David's house. They were told to kill David when he came out the next morning. But Michal, David's wife, warned him, "If you don't escape tonight, you will be dead by morning." So she helped him climb out through a window, and he fled and escaped. Then she took an idol and put it in his bed, covered it with blankets, and put a cushion of goat's hair at its head. When the troops came to arrest David, she told them he was sick and couldn't get out of bed.

1 SAMUEL 18:28–29; 19:11–14

## Pray

*Lord, through the power of your Holy Spirit reveal your truth to me.*

## Observe

There are times in our lives when our convictions are challenged—when friends, loved ones, or acquaintances expect us to participate in conversations or actions that defy the will of God. To walk in true freedom, we must take inventory of our choices and ensure they align with God and his Word. For many of us, it's time to shine healing light on our relational, emotional, and physical boundaries.

A boundary is a personal property line. An invisible marker that helps us make distinctions between what we will allow in our lives and what we won't.

Michal was the daughter of King Saul and the wife of David. Bent on killing her husband, her father had his men surround their home. But Michal's loyalty was to David, a man after God's own heart. She stood firm in her conviction to protect her husband, established a boundary with her wicked father, and protected David by helping him escape.

Courageously evaluate your boundaries by asking yourself the following questions.

1. Have I clearly defined my boundaries at work, home, and with friends?
2. Are my boundaries too lenient or too harsh?
3. Have I clearly communicated my boundaries with others?
4. Is it time for me to redefine my boundaries?

## Interpret

God established moral values and clearly communicates right from wrong in his Word. He expects his followers to establish healthy boundaries and stand firm against those who entice others to sin.

## Apply

Pray and ask God to reveal areas in your life today where you need to protect your morals and stand firm in your convictions.

## Pray

*Father, reveal areas in my life where I need to say no or establish healthy boundaries. Give me the courage to stand up for what's right according to your Word and help me make necessary changes in my everyday life.*

# LET THE BIBLE COME ALIVE

## (AIMEE SEMPLE MCPHERSON)

For the word of God is alive and powerful. It is sharper than the sharpest two-edged sword, cutting between soul and spirit, between joint and marrow. It exposes our innermost thoughts and desires.

HEBREWS 4:12

### Pray

Lord, help me develop a deeper desire for you as I encounter your Word.

### Observe

What role does the Bible play in your life? A source of inspiration and hope? A resource for your relationship with God? Or simply a book that lies quietly on an end table, patiently awaiting your attention?

By letting the Bible come alive in our lives, we nurture our relationship with God and establish a foundation that strengthens our ability to maintain a hopeful attitude and persevere in trying times. The Bible provides the single greatest source of wisdom and guidance for every life circumstances.

When we first surrender our lives to Christ, our primary focus is on our eternal destination. Too often, we stop there and neglect to realize there's more to be explored and a transformed life to be lived—if we will simply let the Bible come alive.

Aimee Semple McPherson preached the gospel to her dolls as a child before she became a popular evangelist in the United States in the 1920s and '30s. It is said that people loved her because she made the Bible come alive. Aimee developed creative ways to illustrate her sermons, and people traveled hundreds of miles just to hear her preach. In an era when women were not even allowed to vote, she refused to ignore God's calling on her life. Aimee founded the International Church of the Foursquare Gospel, with over two million members and close to 30,000 churches worldwide, and she became the first woman to ever preach the gospel on the radio.

Courageously let the Bible come alive in your life by accepting the following truths.

1. Study God's Word for guidance and direction in life (Psalm 119:105).
2. Study God's Word for wisdom (James 1:5).
3. Study God's Word to protect your heart and mind (Romans 12:2).

4. Study God's Word to learn and
   grow spiritually (2 Timothy 3:16).

## Interpret

The Bible is active and alive. It exposes the good, bad, and ugly within us and helps us grow into the faithful followers of Christ we are called to be.

## Apply

Do you treat God's Word as if it's a source of life to you? Name one way you will incorporate Scripture into your life today.

## Pray

*Father, your Word gives wisdom, direction, and life. It teaches me about you, and it helps me clean up my life. Allow me to hunger and thirst for you and for a daily dose of your Word.*

# EXPRESS TRUE REPENTANCE

## (WOMAN WHO ANOINTED JESUS)

When a certain immoral woman from that city heard he was eating there, she brought a beautiful alabaster jar filled with expensive perfume. Then she knelt behind him at his feet, weeping. Her tears fell on his feet, and she wiped them off with her hair. Then she kept kissing his feet and putting perfume on them. … "I tell you, her sins—and they are many—have been forgiven, so she has shown me much love. But a person who is forgiven little shows only little love." Then Jesus said to the woman, "Your sins are forgiven."

LUKE 7:37–38, 47–48

## Pray

*Lord, prepare my heart and mind and give me a teachable spirit.*

## Observe

When children disappoint and disobey their parents, they are often told to say, "I'm sorry." A mother may say to her son, "Tell your sister you are sorry." And her son may fight and fidget until she is forced to ask him again. Finally, the little boy voices those two simple words, "I'm sorry," realizing he must do as he is told to continue playing and to avoid punishment.

Have you ever watched a scenario like this and witnessed the lack of genuine remorse? How often, as adults, do we do the same thing? To avoid conflict and to keep the peace, we often quickly apologize and say, "I'm sorry," without being truly remorseful.

In Luke chapter 7, a sinful woman showed up unannounced at the house of Simon. As she approached Jesus, she dropped to her knees and began to wash his feet with her tears. Out of remorse for her sin, this woman kissed her Savior and anointed his feet. In response, Jesus praised her genuine repentance, gladly received her heartfelt gift, and forgave her sins.

Courageously express true repentance by practicing the following.

1. Ask God to help you identify your sins and give you the courage to admit them.
2. Humble yourself before God and genuinely express your grief over your sins.
3. Ask God to forgive you and help you overcome your sins.
4. Admit your sins to those you've hurt and genuinely ask for their forgiveness.

## Interpret

Christ is moved by compassion and is eager to forgive our sins when we approach him with a humble attitude and a truly repentant heart.

## Apply

Is there a sin you've not confessed or sought forgiveness for? Embrace a truly repentant spirit today, admit your sins, ask God for forgiveness, and seek forgiveness from those you've hurt.

## Pray

*Father, thank you for forgiving my sins and cleansing my unrighteousness. Give me the strength to face my sins with honesty and the courage to ask forgiveness both from you and those I've offended.*

# SERVE FAITHFULLY

## (MARY OF ROME)

Greet my dear friend Epenetus. He was the first person from the province of Asia to become a follower of Christ. Give my greetings to Mary, who has worked so hard for your benefit. Greet Andronicus and Junia, my fellow Jews, who were in prison with me. They are highly respected among the apostles and became followers of Christ before I did.

ROMANS 16:5–7

## Pray

*Lord, open my heart and mind to the needs of others.*

## Observe

God created us to be difference-makers; we are to use our gifts, talents, and resources to help meet the needs of others. He expects us to love and care for others in the same way he loves and cares for us. When we volunteer, donate, or deliver a meal to someone in need, we're not only expressing our love for them, but we are also expressing the depth of our love and devotion to God.

As we embrace opportunities to meet the needs of

others and experience God working in and through us, our faith increases, and our confidence grows. As we employ our God-given gifts and passions, we focus less on our day-to-day issues and begin to appreciate our many blessings on a much deeper level.

Through Christ, God came to earth to express his love for us through serving. Christ healed, he ministered, and he even gave his life in order to provide a pathway to eternity for us. "For even the Son of Man came not to be served but to serve others and to give his life as a ransom for many" (Mark 10:45).

The apostle Paul never missed an opportunity to greet and acknowledge those who served alongside him. In his letter to the Romans, Paul sent greetings to his sister in Christ, Mary, who zealously served believers in Rome.

Courageously challenge your willingness to serve by asking yourself the following questions.

1. Am I using the unique gifts and talents God gave me to serve others? (1 Peter 4:10)
2. Am I encouraging and inspiring others in their faith walk? (Hebrews 10:24–25)
3. Am I willing to serve others without expecting anything in return? (Acts 20:35)
4. Am I serving others with an attitude of patience and love? (Galatians 5:13–14)

## Interpret

God expects us to love and serve others through an outpouring of our love and dedication to him.

## Apply

In what ways are you currently serving others? Ask God to place someone in your path today that you can serve and embrace the opportunity to serve that individual.

## Pray

*Father, grant me a servant's heart and a willingness to faithfully serve you and others. Help me recognize opportunities you provide and inspire me to embrace them with confidence and enthusiasm.*

# WRITE IT DOWN

### (HARRIET BEECHER STOWE)

We proclaim to you what we ourselves have actually seen and heard so that you may have fellowship with us. And our fellowship is with the Father and with his Son, Jesus Christ. We are writing these things so that you may fully share our joy.

1 John 1:3–4

## Pray

*Lord, fill me with awe and wonder as I study your Word and meditate on your precepts.*

## Observe

God used writing as a means to communicate truth to us through the Bible. When we use writing as a means to comfort and encourage others, we are obeying God's command to comfort others with the same comfort we ourselves have been given (2 Corinthians 1:3–4).

Not only is writing a vehicle God uses to help us grow both spiritually and emotionally, but it also allows us to share our stories with others and inspire them to take courageous steps to change their lives. Our stories of courage and unwavering faith prompt others to follow our lead. But our stories of pain and failure also help others as they realize our journey is not one paved with perfection. We are real people with real problems who others can relate to and be encouraged by.

Often, the act of putting feelings into words helps us realize when we are over or under-reacting to our situation, and it affords us the opportunity to think though our experiences and our testimonies. This helps us view our circumstances more objectively and provides a more hopeful and helpful message to those with whom we are sharing.

Harriet Beecher Stowe used writing to inform and inspire her readers with truth. In writing her book *Uncle Tom's Cabin*, she was instrumental in informing the world about the cruel conditions African Americans experienced under slavery. President Abraham Lincoln even suggested her book was a contributing factor to the start of the Civil War.

Courageously write your inspired thoughts by implementing one or more of the following practices.

1. Journal your daily prayers and record the dates and ways in which they are answered.
2. Write about problems you encounter and resolutions God gives you.

3. Journal your life experiences and how your life has been transformed by Christ.
4. Write notes, letters, or devotions that comfort and encourage others.

## Interpret

When we write about the things we have seen and experienced in our Christian journey, we develop fellowship with others and share truth that transforms lives.

## Apply

Express your love and gratitude today by writing a love letter to God.

## Pray

*Father, thank you for inspiring writers to write your words for us to read. Give me inspiration to write, that I may also encourage others to grow in their dedication and devotion to you.*

# SHOW APPRECIATION

### (PHOEBE)

I commend to you our sister Phoebe, who is a deacon in the church in Cenchrea. Welcome her in the Lord as one who is worthy of honor among God's people. Help her in whatever she needs, for she has been helpful to many, and especially to me.

ROMANS 16:1–2

### *Pray*

*Lord, give me a heart of understanding and a genuine desire for a deeper knowledge of you.*

### *Observe*

How often do we recognize and honor the sacrifices and contributions of our brothers and sisters in Christ? More often than not, we are quick to judge, criticize, and complain about those who have dedicated their lives to serving the church, rather than thoughtfully considering the difficulty of their positions and the personal challenges they may face.

Ministry workers are often stretched thin, and some walk away simply burned out. Rarely are they given the benefit of the doubt or shown deserved appreciation. It's common for preachers, teachers, staff, and lay leaders to suffer from discouragement and depression. Therefore, it's vital we find effective ways to honor their work and express our heartfelt appreciation.

"Dear brothers and sisters, honor those who are your leaders in the Lord's work. They work hard among you and give you spiritual guidance. Show them great respect and wholehearted love because of their work. And live peacefully with each other" (1 Thessalonians 5:12–13).

Throughout Paul's many letters, he regularly recognized and celebrated the contributions of his fellow workers in the faith. In Romans chapter 16, Paul praises Phoebe, a fellow laborer and deacon of her church. He encourages the congregation in Rome to welcome Phoebe and help her however they can.

Courageously show appreciation to those who serve the body of Christ by practicing the following.

1. Personally thank and affirm those who volunteer and work in your church.
2. Host a dinner to honor those who dedicate time and resources to God's kingdom work.
3. Write thank-you notes to those who give their time and talents to serve the body of Christ.

4. Volunteer your time and talents to help
carry the load of a ministry worker.

## Interpret

God wants us to honor those who labor for his
kingdom and help them in any way we can.

## Apply

How often do you show appreciation and help
fellow workers in the faith? Take time today to consider
the sacrifice many make in order to serve in ministry
and write a thank-you note to a servant you know
personally.

## Pray

*Father, thank you for the many men and women*
*you call into full-time and part-time ministry. Open*
*my eyes to the sacrifices they make and remind me to*
*always show gratitude for their service.*

# STOP HIDING

## (EVE)

When the cool evening breezes were blowing, the man and his wife heard the Lord God walking about in the garden. So they hid from the Lord God among the trees. Then the Lord God called to the man, "Where are you?" He replied, "I heard you walking in the garden, so I hid. I was afraid because I was naked."

GENESIS 3:8–10

## Pray

*Lord, teach me from your Word and help me walk in your ways.*

## Observe

At some point, we've all worn masks to hide our real selves from the outside world. In fact, we often go to painstaking efforts to construct a captivating masquerade so others might see the person we think they want us to be.

Whether we show our true identity to others or not, Christ knows who you are. He sees our good and our bad—and he still loves us unconditionally and eternally. Jesus is calling us to lay aside our pretense and trust him with our true character. He wants us to confess our weaknesses, sins, and failures so he can cover them and make us whole again. As Johnny Hunt says, "Any sin you cover, God uncovers. Any sin you uncover, God covers."

God wants to reveal the broken places in our lives that motivate us to cover up. He wants us to share our burdens, concerns, and issues with other believers who will pray for us, support us, and love us unconditionally.

Adam and Eve were ashamed of their sin and afraid of God; therefore they hid themselves in the garden. But God, in his abundant mercy and grace, lovingly covered them with animal skin and revealed his plan of redemption through Christ.

Courageously stop hiding your true self:

1. Ask God to help you identity the areas of your life you are covering up.
2. Make a list of the ways you hide your true self from others.
3. Describe the pain and problems that likely cause you to wear masks.
4. Reach out to a godly friend and share your struggles with transparency.

## Interpret

God sees our true character even when we try to hide it. He calls us to come out of hiding and let him cover us through the blood of his sacrifice and his unconditional love.

## Apply

Take one step today to begin removing your masks. Reach out to a safe friend, confess your sins and struggles, and ask for prayer.

## Pray

*Father, no creature is hidden from your sight, and you are very aware of my challenges. Please help me to stop hiding and give me courage to connect with godly friends who will support me as I embrace my true identity.*

# EMBRACE AN "AHA" MOMENT

## (CHRISTINE CAINE)

For I am about to do something new. See, I have already begun! Do you not see it? I will make a pathway through the wilderness. I will create rivers in the dry wasteland.

Isaiah 43:19

## Pray

*Lord, open the eyes of my heart and help me discern truth from your Word.*

## Observe

With work, hobbies, and so many things to distract us, it's easy to miss the aha moments God lovingly sends our way. If we're observant and pay close attention to our surroundings, we will experience moments with God that will captivate our attention—when out of the blue, we discover something that pierces our hearts and draws us toward a new direction. We must be willing to consider that those moments could be a calling from God.

An aha moment is an opportunity from God to begin something new, something that captures our hearts and fulfills his will; an assignment that only he can empower us to accomplish. Like the many men and women of the Bible who've gone before us and have followed God's lead, we must always be prepared and willing to seize the opportunity, even if it means we have to change our direction.

Following God and fulfilling his purposes brings adventure to our lives and joy to our souls.

Is God trying to get your attention? Has he stopped you in your tracks and asked you to embrace a new assignment?

Christine Caine is an evangelist, motivational speaker, and founder of an organization that works tirelessly to dismantle sex trafficking. While in Greece, Christine's heart was pierced by God as she noticed many handmade posters of missing girls. As she investigated the reason so many girls had vanished, she discovered reports of children, even infants, being sold at auctions. Christine decided to use her passion and influence to help rescue victims from this horrific imprisonment.

Courageously embrace your aha moments by adopting the following practices.

1. Keep your eyes on Christ and his will for your life.
2. Pay attention to your surroundings and be open to prompting by the Holy Spirit.

3. Keep your heart, hands, and mind open to new opportunities to serve God.
4. Pray in the spirit at all times about all things.

## Interpret

God creates new things for his people; things that are unexpected and can surpass anything he's done before.

## Apply

Ask God today for an aha moment, one that gets your attention and makes clear the path God wants you to take.

## Pray

*Father, I'm grateful you get my attention in order to lead me in the way you want me to go. Please help me recognize your calling and give me the courage to pursue your will.*

# HAVE AN ETERNAL FOCUS

## (MARTHA)

"Yes," Martha said, "he will rise when everyone else rises, at the last day." Jesus told her, "I am the resurrection and the life. Anyone who believes in me will live, even after dying. Everyone who lives in me and believes in me will never ever die. Do you believe this, Martha?" "Yes, Lord," she told him. "I have always believed you are the Messiah, the Son of God, the one who has come into the world from God."

JOHN 11:24–27

## *Pray*

*Lord, help me see life from your perspective and then live in light of it.*

## *Observe*

Do you believe the words of Jesus? Do you accept the reality that through Christ you will live eternally? Storms, both emotional and physical, can leave us anxious, frustrated, and fearfully focused on the here and now. Or they can motivate us to adopt an eternal perspective.

When tragedy strikes, we naturally run for shelter, and the safest place we can be is in the loving arms of our Savior, Jesus Christ—the one who offers peace, comfort, hope, and reassurance at all times.

Ecclesiastes 3:11 says that God put eternity in our hearts. Therefore, we instinctively long to understand and embrace the reality of our eternal life with God. But as we wait for that future to unfold, we need to face our everyday life circumstances with an eternal perspective.

Early Christians were able to experience joy in their hearts in the midst of trials, crises, and suffering because they chose to place their focus on God rather than their circumstances. In the same way Jesus encouraged Martha to believe that her brother Lazarus would live again, he calls us to make the same declaration of faith.

When we embrace an eternal focus, we view life differently and face our struggles with a courageous and positive attitude.

Embrace these truths and adopt an eternal focus.

1. We can embrace joy in the midst of suffering.
2. We can persevere through hard times, and others will take notice.
3. We can pursue God's calling in spite of difficult circumstances.
4. We can be grateful and content with what we have.

## Interpret

Jesus wants us to fully embrace eternal life and allow it to influence our perspective and outlook on both our current circumstances and our future.

## Apply

Are you currently worried, anxious, frustrated, or afraid as a result of a life situation? Are you willing to give God your struggle today and place your focus on eternity over the worries of today?

## Pray

*Father, help me to embrace an eternal focus and show me areas in my life that I need to surrender to you in order to adopt this new perspective.*

# CHOOSE TO CHANGE

## (PRISCILLA)

Give my greetings to Priscilla and Aquila, my co-workers in the ministry of Christ Jesus. In fact, they once risked their lives for me. I am thankful to them, and so are all the Gentile churches. Also give my greetings to the church that meets in their home.

ROMANS 16:3–5

### Pray

*Lord, remove my distractions and help me focus on truth from your Word.*

### Observe

God often calls us to make courageous changes in life to pursue his God-given calling.

There are hosts of activities and behaviors God calls us to abandon so we can embrace integrity and dedicate our lives to his kingdom work. Because negative actions and attitudes adversely impact our emotional, physical, and spiritual health—and the emotional, physical, and spiritual health of others—we must take the time to identify the changes God is calling us to make so we can pursue the life he is calling us to live.

It is said, "Watch your thoughts, they become words; Watch your words, they become actions; Watch your actions, they become habits; Watch your habits, they become character; Watch your character, for it becomes your destiny."

Priscilla and Aquila chose to take time away from their professions to pursue their God-given purpose and calling. They were both eager to open up their home, travel to foreign lands, and even risk their lives for the sake of the gospel.

Put the following disciplines into practice and begin making courageous changes right away.

1. Pray for wisdom and discernment regarding changes you need to make. Remember that there is no condemnation for those who are in Christ Jesus (Romans 8:1), but the Holy Spirit will convict us of specific things we need to change (John 16:8).

2. Make a list of any attitudes, activities, or behaviors you sense God calling you to change.

3. List at least two positive steps you can take right away to begin making necessary changes.

4. Share your decision to change with a godly friend who will pray for you, encourage

you, and hold you accountable as you
strive to change.

## Interpret

God wants us to make his work a priority in our
lives. Therefore, we need to do whatever is necessary;
even if we are being called to set aside our professions
to pursue his kingdom work and calling.

## Apply

Is there an attitude, behavior, or habit keeping you
from pursuing God's call on your life? What one change
can you make today to remove an obstacle and embrace
God's calling?

## Pray

*Father, thank you for loving me unconditionally
and eternally. Please lead me to make courageous
changes that will allow me to pursue a life that is
pleasing to you and healthy for me.*

# BE BOLD

## (BARBARA BUSH)

For the next two years, Paul lived in Rome at his own expense.
He welcomed all who visited him, boldly proclaiming the
Kingdom of God and teaching about the Lord Jesus Christ. And
no one tried to stop him.

ACTS 28:30–31

## *Pray*

*Lord, give me focus and direction as I study your
Word.*

## *Observe*

Do you get defensive when others attempt to
share truth with you? Or do you find it hard to share the
truth when you believe it will be difficult for others to
receive?

We all experience times in our lives when we
struggle to accept the truth, and we've all been tempted
to fall into the trap of telling someone what they want to
hear, or simply saying nothing at all. But what we often
forget is sugarcoating the truth helps no one, especially
the person we are sprinkling it on.

When we encounter a conflict or issue with another person, God calls us to courageously speak truth in love and receive truth from them (Ephesians 4:15). Unless someone is honest with us and makes us aware of our false beliefs, we're doomed to repeat our same mistakes and continue our same behaviors.

Jesus tells us, "And you will know the truth, and the truth will set you free" (John 8:32). This is true every day of our lives. Even though the truth can sometimes be hard to give and receive, it can usher in emotional, relational, and spiritual freedom when we fearlessly choose to speak it and courageously decide to embrace it.

Former First Lady Barbara Bush, wife of former President George H. W. Bush and mother to former President George W. Bush, was a woman of great faith and conviction. She was known for her candor and wit and never hesitated to share what was on her heart and mind. Barbara was a lifelong volunteer for charitable causes. She spoke boldly against illiteracy and dedicated many years of her life to promoting reading as a priority in America.

Courageously share truth with others boldly and with confidence.

1. Prepare to share the truth in a loving way.

2. Begin the conversation by communicating care for the other person.
3. Remain humble and patient when sharing the truth.
4. Pray and ask God to help the other person receive, understand, and accept the truth.

## Interpret

God expects us to proclaim the gospel and his kingdom with boldness to all who will listen.

## Apply

Initiate a conversation with someone today and boldly share your faith in God and his love for them.

## Pray

*Father, I am grateful for your love that envelops me day after day. Give me courage to speak boldly of your life-saving grace and prompt me to share hope with others who desperately need you.*

# ABOUT THE AUTHOR

**Ann White** is an internationally known author, speaker, and passionate Bible teacher. She founded her global ministry, Courage For Life, out of a calling to share with others how God and His Word brought restoration to her life and marriage. Having personally experienced God's grace, salvation, and the life-changing power of the Bible, Ann's desire is to extend this same love, mercy, and encouragement to others so they too may be reconciled to God.

Ann is a wife, mother, and grandmother. She and her husband reside in Belleair Shores, Florida.

Learn more about Ann and her ministry, Courage For Life, at CourageForLife.org and on Facebook, Twitter, Instagram, Pinterest, and YouTube @AnnWhiteCFL.

courageforlife.org